THE
UFO-CHRISTIANITY
CONNECTION

Fact or Fiction

Fred R. David, PhD

iUniverse, Inc.
New York   Bloomington

The UFO–Christianity Connection
Fact or Fiction

iUniverse books may be ordered through booksellers or by contacting:

iUniverse
1663 Liberty Drive
Bloomington, IN 47403
www.iuniverse.com
1-800-Authors (1-800-288-4677)

ISBN: 978-1-4502-6561-4 (pbk)
ISBN: 978-1-4502-6562-1 (cloth)
ISBN: 978-1-4502-6563-8 (ebk)

Library of Congress Control Number: 2010916057

Printed in the United States of America

iUniverse rev. date: 11/4/2010

www.ufochristianityconnection.com

Direct All Inquiries To:
Fred R. David, Ph.D.
Freddavid9@gmail.com

To my editorial, production, and marketing manager for this book - my wife for thirty-two years and best friend for life, Joy David.

List of Illustrations

(attributions given at end of book)

1) Front Cover: *"The Madonna with Saint Giovannino"*

2) Picture of the Author

3) UFO in Wales Picture

4) Two Images of UFOs:
   a. Sheffield, England, March 4, 1962
   b. Minneapolis, Minnesota, October 20, 1960

5) Vatican Observatory Picture

6) Possible Routes of the Exodus

7) A Depiction of Jacob's Ladder

8) Great Pyramid of Giza Picture

9) Great Sphinx Picture

10) Sumeria Map

11) Commonly Accepted Depiction of a Neanderthal Male

12) A Skull Comparison: Homo Sapiens Left, Neanderthal Right

13) The City of Cuzco, Peru as it Looks Today

14) Lake Titicaca Map

15) Nazca Lines

16) The Olmec Empire

17) Stonehenge as it Looked in the 1600s

18) Easter Island

19) Aztec Empire in the Year 1519

20) A Mayan Temple at Chichen Itza

21) Mayan Long Count Calendar

22) Indus Valley Map

23) A Picture of Edgar Cayce in 1910

24) A Painting of Plato

25) Map Showing Lemuria and Atlantis

26) A Mammoth

27) Giant Human's Femur Bone

28) Color Coded North America Map of Bigfoot Sightings

29) A Solar Flare

30) The Russian Yamantau Mountain Complex

31) The Svalbard Global Seed Vault Near the North Pole

32) Mount Tabor

33) *The Baptism of Christ* – A 1710 Painting by Aert De Gelder

34) July 2010 China UFO (pic1)

35) July 2010 China UFO (pic2)

36) *The Annunciation* – A 1486 AD Painting by Carlo Crivelli

37) *The Annunciation* – A 1434 AD Painting by Jan van Eyck

38) Commonly Accepted Depiction of Jesus Christ – This is a painting of Jesus at the "Basilica of Saint'Apollinare Nuovo" in Ravenna, Italy: *"Christ Surrounded By Angels and Saints."* A Mosaic of a Ravennate Italian-Byzantine Workshop, (Completed about 526 AD by the "Master of Saint'Apollinare").

Acknowledgments

Thank you reviewers of this book, especially Dave and Kathy Cyrulik, George and Shirley Everhart, Joy David, Forest David, Meredith David, Byron and Brooke David, Bruce and Kathy Williams, Phillip and Anne David, Dr. Ed Ramirez, Vern Bender, Joni Pederson, JoAnn Smock, and Jim Padgett. Thank you also to creators of all public domain pictures included in this book. Thank you Joe Taylor, director of the Mt. Blanco Fossil Museum in Crosbyton, Texas for permission to include the forty-seven-inch human femur picture. Thank you Bruce Lauzon for being my Web site manager and Nick Hempsey who designed the front cover. Thank you, Randall Gillette and Eric Hanselmann and all the persons at iUniverse, for the very professional manner that you do business with authors.

About the Front Cover

This main center picture on the front cover is the famous painting of mother Mary with baby Jesus and the infant St. John. Known as *The Madonna with Saint Giovannino*, this painting was created in the fifteenth century by Domenico Ghirlandaio (1449-1494) and/ or Sebastiano Mainardi (1466-1513). From that painting, note the enlargements where a man and his dog can clearly be seen looking up at a UFO. This painting is on display today in the Sala díErcole Museum in Palazzo Vecchio in Florence, Italy. There are other ancient paintings of Jesus and Mary with UFOs, such as those at: *http://www.cosmicchrist.net/Christian_art_UFO_pictures_aliens_Jesus_ Christ_Mary.htm*

About the Author

Fred R. David, Ph.D is the author of *"Strategic Management: Concepts and Cases"* which has been used at more than four hundred colleges and universities, including Harvard University, Carnegie-Mellon, and Duke University. Translated and published by Prentice Hall in five languages, Dr. David's books have led the field of strategic management for nearly two decades. His textbooks may be seen at *www.prenhall.com/david*.

Fred Davd is author of more than one hundred refereed publications, including many articles in prestigious journals. His recent *"History of Ocean Isle Beach"* book, published by Donning Publishers, may be seen at *www.oceanislehistory.com*. For the last two years, Dr. David has focused time, effort, skills, and interest on ancient history, and conducted extensive research on UFOs and ancient religious writings. His latest research findings are assimilated in *"The UFO-Christianity Connection: Fact or Fiction"* that may be seen at *www.ufochristianityconnection.com*.

Fred David received a BS in mathematics and an MBA degree from Wake Forest University and a PhD in general management from the University of South Carolina. He has served on the faculty at the University of North Carolina at Pembroke, East Carolina University, Mississippi State University, and Auburn University. He currently is a professor of management at Francis Marion University in Florence, South Carolina. He resides in Ocean Isle Beach, North Carolina with his wife Joy. Fred and Joy have three grown children, Forest, Byron, and Meredith, and two beagle dogs, Spikes and Aubie.

Introduction

This book examines evidence across discipline, distance, and time that brings to life the close association that ancient civilizations had with ancient astronauts, which they called gods or sky people. As early humans gazed into the sky at night, they were more certain than mankind today that "we are not alone in the universe." The *Bible* reveals that God expects human beings to think, to strive to become all that we can become, as indicated in Romans 12:2, which says, "And be not conformed to this world: but be ye transformed by the renewing of your mind, that ye may prove what is that good, and acceptable, and perfect, will of God." Thus, this book aims to renew your mind and perhaps strengthen your faith by expanding your knowledge of the UFO-Christianity connection. Simply put, this book aims to reveal the truth. Any true god will represent truth, which is the essence of God, and why God gave us a brain, which is to pursue truth. Ultimately, truth will always win out.

Most people every day conduct their lives with an understanding of religion based largely on what they were taught as a children or adolescents by their parents, family, and friends. This is generally a good thing, but being open-minded to new discoveries and knowledge is important. Walking around uninformed or uninterested is not good considering how important the implications may be for life, or even eternal life. Blind faith in Christianity is admirable, but expanding one's knowledge of the UFO-Christianity connection and realizing there may be a scientific basis for events in the *Bible*, may strengthen a person's faith. We all should continually read, study, explore, listen, debate, and watch as more and more pieces of the puzzle of life are uncovered everyday. Examining the UFO-Christianity connection is good, needed among mankind, and could eventually help unite humanity - because all people on earth are almost identical genetically. Only when we gaze into the sky at night do we see the home of beings different than ourselves.

This book examines writings of the Maya, Aztec, Egyptians, Sumerians, and Indians, all of which indicate that UFOs played a significant role in how ancient civilizations lived. People thousands of years ago, for example, somehow built megalithic structures without heavy lifting equipment, predicted celestial events without telescopes, and drew similar pictures all over the planet of sky people. This book examines the UFO connection with many topics in the *Bible* and offers you a unique perspective to engage others in discussion about angels, God, UFOs, Satan, giants, the underworld, the flood, Enoch, Atlantis, Jesus, the Sons of God, the date 12-21-12, and Christianity.

This book examines current knowledge from paleontology, archeology, geology, anthropology, astronomy, physics, and genetics as related to the UFO phenomena. Documented evidence for UFOs is considered from writings, stories, and pictures from ancient civilizations. Substantial evidence suggests that the scientific basis for Judaism, Islam, Hinduism, Buddhism, and other religions may be UFOs – so this book provides valuable information for people of all faiths on all continents. This book in some ways is an extension to Eric Von Daniken's *"Chariots of the Gods."*

As the governing body of the Roman Catholic Church, the Vatican is accelerating its Public Acclimation Program to assure its faithful, and others, that star visitors are real, are in the *Bible*, and are children of God, too. The Vatican's Monsignor Corrado Balducci, just before he died on died September 20, 2008 in Italy, proclaimed on Italian national television that "encounters people have had and do have with star visitors are real, not a delusion, and not a case of demon possession." Balducci also said these star visitors "appear to be more advanced, intellectually and spiritually, than humans." The Vatican's Jesuit Brother Guy Consolmagno, a Harvard- and MIT-trained astronomer with a Ph.D at the Vatican Observatory in Arizona, wrote in the April 2006 issue of *Harper's Magazine*: "There are, unquestionably, nonhuman intelligent beings in the *Bible*." He quoted Jesus as saying, "I have other sheep that do not belong to this fold (John 10: 15-16)."

Then Consolmagno wrote, "And perhaps it's not so far-fetched to see the Second Person of the Trinity not only as the Son of Man but also as a Child of other Races. Any creature in the universe, created and loved by the same God who created and loves us ... Would they deserve to be called alien?" Then Consolmagno wrote, "God is bigger than whatever parallel universes may or may not exist beyond our own. And God is able to concentrate his entire effort, energy and love on each one of us tiny individuals on this tiny planet; and, I have confidence, on any other individuals on any other planet as well."

For many centuries, science and religion have remained staunchly independent.

Whenever issues have developed that simultaneously touched on both areas, arguing often ensured – such as when scientists proposed that the earth rotates around the sun or when evolution was proposed to explain the creation story. There has always been a "missing link" between science and religion that has caused dissention and distrust. However, research conducted for this book reveals that the missing link between science and religion may be UFOs, or more specifically the beings inside those craft. Evidence for a clear UFO-Christianity connection could bring science and religion closer, and perhaps one day into perfect union.

People are naturally intrigued and interested in issues they do not fully understand, such as angels, heaven, hell, ghosts, spirits, giants, miracles, gods, Satan, aliens, the underworld, and God. What is true and what is not true? Living an unexplained existence is uncomfortable at best. For thousands of years, people have yearned for a better understanding of the relationship between the past, present, and future as well as between science and religion. This book reveals that science and religion are actually much more closely intertwined than most people think. As more and more archaeological evidence is uncovered everyday, it becomes clearer and clearer that ancient writings such as the *Bible* are both history and science books. As revealed in this book, the history and science aspects of the *Bible* are corroborated by other ancient writings, such as the *Dead Sea Scrolls*, the Mayan *Popol Vuh*, the Indian *Vedas*, the Aztecs' *Codex Vaticanus*, the Sumerian *Epic of Gilgamesh*, and the *Book of Enoch*. Many events described in ancient writings, including the *Bible*, probably involved UFO encounters.

During biblical times, from say about 2000 BC to 400 AD, God the Father was reportedly present in "clouds and chariots." This book provides a scientific basis for the realization that most if not all events described in the *Bible* indeed happened, some perhaps because God was onsite in a UFO. God's watchers today may use UFOs to monitor humanity as guardian angels. Evidence is presented here that God's watchers may use our moon as home base, and could be responsible for such activities as: (1) answering prayers, (2) performing miracles, (3) managing souls as people die, (4) making sure Satan and the underworld remain in check, (5) keeping God and Jesus informed, and (6) monitoring or influencing world events.

This book provides thirty-eight pictures and more than one hundred examples to bring to life the UFO-Christianity connection. Implications of this evidence for the upcoming 12-21-12 Mayan last day and biblical doctrine are provided. This book is exceptionally up-to-date, concisely written, enjoyable, and presents important information for people of all faiths on all continents. Substantial documentation throughout, including YouTube videos, History Channel documentaries, and Web sites, enable each reader to further explore any topic discussed. This book will help you decide whether the UFO-Christianity connection is fact or fiction.

Chapter 1:
ARE UFOs REAL?

The possibility and nature of unidentified flying objects (UFOs) intrigues nearly everyone. Literally thousands of people over many centuries have seen these craft. You may even have a friend or friends who have seen a UFO. Many airplane pilots, ship captains, police officers, military personnel, and regular citizens worldwide have seen and photographed UFOs. Air traffic control radar towers on numerous occasions have confirmed pilots' visual description of a UFO in range and tracked the craft's speed and direction. Many books document UFO sightings by reliable persons over many centuries.

There are thousands of documented UFO sightings but two recent examples are described below. The first incident occurred on Wednesday night, July 7, 2010 when a UFO flew into the airspace of the Xiaoshan Airport near Hangzhou, the capital of east China's Zhejiang Province. The airport closed all flights in and out from 9:00 PM to 10:00 PM as the UFO was tracked on radar. Around 1:00 AM that evening just after the airport had reopened, Hangzhou residents reported seeing a large, brightly lit, elongated UFO in the sky. A year earlier in July 2009, during the viewing of a solar eclipse in China, scientists at the Purple Mountain Astronomical Observatory in Nanjing filmed forty minutes of a UFO reportedly near the sun. No definitive explanation of either event from the Chinese government has been given. A YouTube video of this recent sighting is provided on the next page:

http://www.dailyfinance.com/story/ufos-over-china-alien-invasion-or-economic-indicator/19559850/?icid=main\main\dl2\link4\http%3A%2F%2Fwww.dailyfinance.com%2Fstory%2Fufos-over-china-alien-invasion-or-economic-indicator%2F19559850%2F

The second incident occurred on June 7, 2008, near Cardiff in Wales, Great Britain. A police helicopter hovering at five hundred feet and, waiting for clearance to land, was forced to take evasive action to avoid a UFO. The helicopter was returning to the Ministry of Defence base at St. Athan when the pilot spotted the UFO coming rapidly towards them. According to the South Wales Police, the helicopter crew crossed the Bristol Channel in pursuit of the UFO, but lost sight of it and was forced to return to base due to low fuel. Since the pilot did not have a camera, a journalist's rendition of what the Wales UFO looked like is provided below:

The June 7, 2008 UFO Seen Near Cardiff in Wales, Great Britain

Source: *http://mathildasweirdworldweblog.wordpress.com/2008/06/22/welsh-ufo-flap-in-progress/*

Some well documented UFO incidents and statements over the last one hundred fifty years are provided below as examples:

* 1879 The U.S.S. *Vulture* crew operating in the Persian Gulf witnessed two luminous rotating wheels, about one hundred thirty feet across. They hovered above the ship and then plunged into the water.

* 1880 The British steamer *Patna* and its crew witnessed two glowing, spinning wheels estimated to be five hundred to six hundred meters in diameter appear underwater on each side of the ship.

* 1897 A cigar-shaped UFO crashed in Aurora, Texas on April 19. A four-foot tall alien was buried in a small north Aurora cemetery.

* 1945 In the Bering Sea off Alaska, the U.S. Army Transport vessel *Delarof* was hauling munitions and supplies to Alaska. The crew saw a large object emerge from the sea. They were able to see the darkness of the craft against the setting sun. The craft climbed almost straight up, leveled off and began to circle the ship. The crew estimated the UFO to be about two hundred feet in diameter. The UFO circled the ship three times, making no sound, and after a few minutes, took off towards the south followed by three flashes of light as the craft disappeared.

* 1947 In Roswell, New Mexico, a UFO crashed. The USA military retrieved several aliens and secretly conducted autopsies on them.

* 1952 From July 13 to July 29, in and around Washington, DC, numerous pilots, traffic controllers, and officials witnessed more than a dozen UFOs.

* 1955 General Douglas MacArthur stated, "The nations of the earth must some day make a common front against attack by people from other planets. MacArthur established the IPU (Interplanetary Phenomenon Unit) to investigate crashed and retrieved UFOs.

* 1960 Dr. Herman Oberth, the father of modern rocketry, said, "It is my thesis that UFOs are real. They are spaceships from another solar system. We cannot take credit for our record advancement in certain

scientific fields alone. We have been helped." When asked who has helped mankind, Oberth replied; "The people of other worlds." Oberth said, "UFOs are conceived and directed by intelligent beings of a very high order. UFOs are propelled by distorting the gravitational field - converting gravity into useable energy. There is no doubt in my mind that these objects are interplanetary craft of some sort."

* 1962 Astronaut Scott Carpenter said, "At no time when we were in space were we alone; there was a constant surveillance by UFOs." Carpenter photographed a UFO while in orbit on May 24, 1962. NASA still has not released the photograph.

* 1968 When asked about UFOs, Robert F. Kennedy said, "As you may know, I am a card-carrying member of the Amalgamated Flying Saucers Association."

* 1968 Astronaut James Lovell, commander of the Apollo 13 mission that orbited the moon, made the following transmission after coming around the far (dark) side of the moon, "Mission Control, please be informed, there is a Santa Claus." (The NASA codeword for a UFO was Santa Claus).

* 1968 On the morning of May 20, three UFOs were reported to rise up out of Moore Lake in Littleton, New Hampshire.

* 1971 Captain Edgar Mitchell, Astronaut on the Apollo 14 moon mission and the sixth man on the moon, said, "The evidence points to the fact that Roswell was a real incident and that indeed an alien craft did crash and that material was recovered from that crash site. We all know that UFOs are real. All we need to ask is where do they come from?"

* 1973 President Jimmy Carter and his son Jeff in Georgia a few years before his run for the presidency watched a UFO for ten minutes. On numerous occasions thereafter, President Jimmy Carter stated, "I am convinced that UFOs exist because I have seen one. I don't laugh at people any more when they say they've seen UFOs."

* 1973 Astronaut Eugene Cernan, who commanded the Apollo 17 mission that landed on the moon, said, "I've been asked about UFOs and I've said publicly I thought they were somebody else, some other civilization."

* 1985 Astronaut Colonel Gordon Cooper, speaking to the United Nations Panel on UFOs and ETs, said, "I believe these extraterrestrial vehicles and their crews are visiting this planet from other planets and are obviously more technically advanced than we are here on Earth. We need a top level, coordinated program to scientifically collect and analyze data from all over the earth concerning any type of encounter, and determine how best to interface with these visitors in a friendly fashion. As far as I am concerned, there have been too many unexplained examples of UFO sightings around earth for us to rule out the possibilities that some form of life exists out there beyond our own world. I know other astronauts share my feelings and we know the government is sitting on hard evidence of UFOs!"

* 1999 In October, Astronaut Neil Armstrong said, "We have no proof, but if we extrapolate, based on the best information we have available to us, we have to come to the conclusion that other life probably exists out there and perhaps in many places."

* 2000 John Glenn said, "I believe certain reports of flying saucers to be legitimate."

Despite extensive evidence that UFOs exist, governments worldwide have apparently agreed to cover up their knowledge of UFOs. This cover up may be one of the best examples of global cooperation among countries today. Stephen Bassett, the only registered UFO lobbyist in Washington, DC, has been working for years to get the US government to release information confirming the existence of alien beings visiting earth. In the February 2010 issue of *Washington Monthly*, Mr. Bassett says President Obama may be on the verge of disclosing UFO information. This three-page-news article is provided at the Web site: http://www. washingtonmonthly.com/features/2010/1001.tms-fromson.html

In the following four-minute video, American astronauts and Stephen

Bassett discuss the truth regarding UFOs and their contact with people and governments. Mr. Bassett argues for disclosing information that reveals the presence of alien beings.
http://www.youtube.com/watch?v=-gO4aYKVkB8

In the following ten-minute video, Steven Greer, an American physician, author, lecturer and founder of the Orion Project and The Disclosure Project, introduces twenty different NASA, CIA, Army, Navy, and Air Force experts who give testimony regarding the presence of extraterrestrials on earth and the alleged government cover-up.
http://www.youtube.com/watch?v=NCKoQ6FWyM4

Proponents of the Disclosure Project say UFO propulsion technology could replace fossil fuels and thus benefit mankind immensely. The following fifty-nine minute video reveals extensive testimony by experts describing classified UFO information.
http://video.google.com/videoplay?docid=6552475158249898710#

Similar to Area 51 near Groom Lake, Nevada, but located more than two thousand miles away, is the US Navy's top secret Atlantic Undersea Test and Evaluation Center (AUTEC). Located on the southeast corner of the Bermuda Triangle where planes and ships have disappeared, AUTEC includes three test ranges: the Weapons Range, the Acoustic Range, and the FORACS Range. These ranges are located in the Tongue of the Ocean (TOTO), a deep-ocean basin approximately one hundred nautical miles long by fifteen nautical miles wide with depths as great as six thousand feet. The Weapons Range is capable of tracking up to sixty-three in-water objects simultaneously and provides AN/WQC-2A Sonar Communications Sets and Bi-Directional Communications Nodes for underwater voice communications with mobile underwater objects at extreme depths. AUTEC's in-air tracking is provided by radar and other systems out five-hundred nautical miles and to a height of seventy-thousand feet.

Located on Andros Island in the Bahamas just west of Nassau, AUTEC former employees speak on the eight-minute History Channel video below. Several AUTEC scientists and researchers reveal on the video

that the United States monitors UFOs coming and going from ocean depths near the AUTEC facility.
http://www.ufo-blogger.com/2009/05/history-channel-ufo-hunters-navy.html

Three primary reasons for the worldwide government cover up may be as follows:

1. Governments believe acknowledging the existence of UFOs would cause extensive social unrest and upheaval.
2. Governments obtain national security information from UFO crashes and behavior, including advanced technologies and potential weapon systems.
3. UFO technology is so far advanced from our own that there is nothing anyone could do anyway to prevent UFOs from doing whatever they desire.

Former Special Assistant to the Deputy Director of the CIA Victor Marchetti, may be absolutely right when he said, "We have, indeed, been contacted – perhaps even visited – by extraterrestrial beings, and the U.S. government, in collusion with the other national powers of the earth, is determined to keep this information from the general public. The purpose of the international conspiracy is to maintain a workable stability among the nations of the world and for them, in turn, to retain institutional control over their respective populations. Thus, for these governments to admit that there are beings from outer space with mentalities and technological capabilities obviously far superior to ours, could, once fully perceived by the average person, erode the foundations of the earth's traditional power structure. Political and legal systems, religions, economic and social institutions could all soon become meaningless in the mind of the public. National establishments, even civilization as we now know it, could collapse into anarchy." (*Second Look*, Vol. 1, No. 7, May 1979).

Ancient writings, stories, carvings, and pictures indicate that advanced beings from somewhere in the universe have consistently visited earth for thousands of years. Some kind of being obviously is inside the UFOs. Whether you call that entity an alien, god, extraterrestrial, ancient astronaut, or Marsian, UFOs have been chased for miles by pilots and police officers and tracked by both military and civilian air controllers. UFOs can go from a speed of zero to over seven thousand mph within seconds, and then instantly come to a dead stop, or climb vertically out of sight in a one second. Clearly this technology is not from this world. These craft have been described as being only ten feet in diameter to nearly two thousand feet. Some are cigar shaped but most are oval. A large UFO hovering or moving slowly on a sunny day, such as the Wales UFO, would cast shade on the ground, like a cloud.

Two images of UFOs that once were included on the CIA website are given on the next page. The first picture was taken on March 4, 1962 in Sheffield, England. The second picture was taken on October 20, 1960 in Minneapolis, Minnesota.

UFOs: Top Picture - Taken on March 4, 1962 in Sheffield, England
Bottom Picture – Taken on October 20,
1960 in Minneapolis, Minnesota

Source: *http://en.wikipedia.org/wiki/File:P70.gif and the CIA Web site Page: (https://www.cia.gov/library/center-for-the-study-of-intelligence/csi-publications/csi-studies/studies/97unclass/ufo. html) Image: (https://www.cia.gov/library/center-for-the-study-of-intelligence/csi-publications/csi-studies/studies/97unclass/p70.gif)*
Note: Wikipedia says this image is a work of a CIA employee, taken or made during the course of an employee's official duties. As a work of the U.S. federal government, the image is in the public domain.

A reasonable conclusion is that UFOs truly do exist and have been observed for thousands of years. Too many reliable people all over the world have reported seeing a UFO, often many persons at the same time. Documented UFO sightings, crashes, and landings in many countries across the globe over many centuries are too compelling to deny the existence of UFOs visiting earth from somewhere. To simply tell all eyewitnesses they were mistaken is becoming more and more politically incorrect rather than correct.

It may be debated as to why UFOs visit earth, or where they come from, or how they operate, or how long they have been here, or who is at the helm, but skeptics perhaps should consider moving beyond denial of UFOs and forward to deciphering for what purpose do these craft visit earth. When you go for your next afternoon or evening walk, be looking up rather than always at the ground, because you could become the next eyewitness to a UFO. The reality of UFOs from eyewitness accounts provides a basis for us to examine the UFO-*Bible* connection next.

Chapter 2:
THE UFO-BIBLE CONNECTION

The central governing body of the Roman Catholic Church is the Vatican. In May 2008, the Vatican publicly acknowledged for the first time that "intelligent life may exist on other planets and the possibility of extraterrestrial life is compatible with Christian ideology." One of the oldest astronomical research institutions in the world is the Vatican Observatory, headquartered at the papal summer residence in Castel Gandolfo, Italy outside Rome. A picture of the Observatory is provided on the next page:

Fred R. David, PhD

The Vatican Observatory Near Rome, Italy

Source: *http://en.wikipedia.org/wiki/Vatican_Observatory*

The Vatican Observatory Research Group at the University of Arizona in Tucson operates the huge Alice P. Lennon Telescope with its Thomas J. Bannan Astrophysics Facility, known together as the Vatican Advanced Technology Telescope (VATT). Director of the Vatican Observatory, George Coyne, for twenty-eight minutes at the Web site *http://www.youtube.com/watch?v=wHqxlj_n-nk* discusses the purpose of the observatory and the nature of science and religion. Dr. Coyne has a PhD in Astronomy and is a Catholic priest.

The Vatican is clearly interested in astrophysics and astronomy and actively supports the continued dialogue between faith and science.

Pope John Paul II wrote the following in a letter to George Coyne on June 1, 1988: "Only a dynamic relationship between theology and science can reveal those limits which support the integrity of either discipline, so that theology does not profess a pseudo-science and science does not become an unconscious theology. Our knowledge of each other can lead us to be more authentically ourselves. We need each other to be what we must be, what we are called to be."

In addition to eyewitness and crash evidence for UFOs gathered over the last few centuries, the existence of these craft becomes even more certain when one reads ancient writings, including the *Bible*. More than eight hundred *Bible* verses use terms like flying, hovering, spinning, ascending, descending, landing, flashing, metallic, and glowing to describe "chariots or wheels" in the sky. Many scholars believe these verses refer to UFOs, similar to those periodically seen today.

Persons in the *Bible* who witnessed or mentioned flying vehicles include Moses, Samuel, Job, Ezra, Elijah, Elisha, Joshua, Jonah, Jeremiah, Solomon, Nehemiah, Isaiah, Ezekiel, Daniel, Joel, Amos, Habakkuk, Nahum, Yephaniah, Zechariah, Matthew, Mark, Luke, John, Peter, James, Paul, and Jesus. The *Bible* says Jesus will be in charge of twenty thousand chariots when he returns at the Second Coming. Even the *Quran* says Jesus will return in this manner.

Flying vehicles in the *Bible* were often referred to as "clouds" that provide "shade during the day" and "amber or fiery lights at night." Writers of the *Bible* and observers during biblical days also referred to these vehicles as platforms, chariots, sky thrones, whirlwinds, and wheels, often describing them as moving extremely fast, or hovering, ascending, or descending.

In the year 593 BC, according to the *Bible*, the prophet Ezekiel "went up into Heaven in a whirlwind." Ezekiel was one of the most significant prophets in the *Bible* and while sitting at the river Chabur, near Nippur, in present day Iraq, Ezekiel suddenly saw a "fiery whirlwind" moving fast towards him. Josef Blumrich, former chief of the systems layout branch of NASA, studied the Ezekiel historical accounts and concluded that the vehicle described in the *Bible* actually was a UFO.

A few *Bible* verses are provided below that use the words *"clouds,"* *"chariots,"* *"wheel,"* or *"whirlwind."* As you read through the sample verses, consider whether you think Moses, Samuel, Job, Ezra, Elijah, Elisha, Joshua, Jonah, Jeremiah, Solomon, Nehemiah, Isaiah, Ezekiel, Daniel, Joel, Amos, Habakkuk, Nahum, Yephaniah, Zechariah, Matthew, Mark, Luke, John, Peter, James, Paul, and Jesus were mistaken or delusional in what they were seeing and reporting. How better could someone back then describe a UFO?

Psalms 68:17 The *chariots* of God are twenty thousand, even thousands of angels: the Lord is among them, as in Sinai, in the holy place.

Deuteronomy 1:33 Who went in the way before you, to search you out a place to pitch your tents in *fire by night*, to show you by what way ye should go, and in a *cloud by day.*

1 Kings 18:44 Behold, there ariseth a little *cloud* out of the sea, like a man's hand.

Isaiah 19:1 Behold, the Lord rideth upon a swift *cloud*, and shall come into Egypt: and the idols of Egypt shall be moved at his presence.

Matthew 17:5 While he yet spake, behold, a bright *cloud* overshadowed them; and behold a voice out of the *cloud*, which said, This is my beloved Son, in whom I am well pleased; hear ye him.

Matthew 24:30 And then shall appear the sign of the Son of man in heaven; and then shall all the tribes of the earth mourn, and they shall see the Son of man coming in the *clouds* of heaven with power and great glory.

Mark 9:7-8 And there was a *cloud* that overshadowed them: and a voice came out of the *cloud*, saying, "This is my beloved Son: hear him." And suddenly, when they had looked round about, they saw no man any more, only Jesus with themselves.

Mark 14:62 And Jesus said, "I am: and ye shall see the Son of man sitting on the right hand of power, and coming in the *clouds* of heaven."

Acts 1:9 And when he had spoken these things, while they beheld, he was taken up; and a *cloud* received him out of their sight.

1 Thessalonians 4:17 Then we which are alive and remain shall be caught up together with them in the *clouds* to meet the Lord in the air; and so shall we ever be with the Lord.

Revelation 1:7 Behold, he cometh with *clouds*; and every eye shall see him.

Revelation 11:11 And they ascended up to heaven in a *cloud*.

Job 38:1 Then the Lord answered Job out of the *whirlwind*, and said ...

2 Kings 2:11 And it came to pass, as they still went on, and talked, that, behold, there appeared a *chariot of fire*, and horses of fire, and parted them both asunder; and Elijah went up by a *whirlwind* into heaven.

2 Kings 2:12 And Elisha saw it, and he cried, My father, my father, the *chariot* of Israel.

Zechariah 6:1 And I turned, and lifted up mine eyes, and looked, and, behold, there came *four chariots* out from between two mountains; and the mountains were mountains of brass.

Isaiah 66:15 For behold, the Lord will come with fire, and with *his chariots like a whirlwind*, to render his anger with fury, and his rebuke with flames of fire.

Genesis 15:17 And it came to pass, that, when the sun went down, and it was dark, behold a smoking furnace, and a *burning lamp that passed over.*

Jeremiah 4:13 Behold, he shall come up as *clouds*, and his *chariots* shall be as a *whirlwind*: his horses are swifter than eagles.

Jeremiah 23:19 Behold, a *whirlwind* of the Lord is gone forth in fury, even a grievous *whirlwind*: it shall fall grievously upon the head of the wicked.

Jeremiah 25:32 Thus saith the Lord of hosts, Behold, evil shall go forth from nation to nation, and a great *whirlwind* shall be raised up from the coasts of the earth.

Psalms 104:3 Who layeth the beams of his chambers in the waters: who maketh the *clouds his chariot*: who walketh upon the wings of the wind.

Mark 16:19 After the Lord had spoken unto them, he was *received up into heaven*, and sat on the right hand of God.

John 20:17 Jesus saith unto Mary, Touch me not; for I am not yet *ascended* to my Father; but go to my brethren, and say unto them, I ascend unto my Father, and your Father; and to my God, and your God.

Acts 1:9 And when he had spoken these things, while they beheld, he was taken up; and a *cloud* received him out of their sight.

Exodus 13:21 And the Lord went before them *by day in a pillar of a cloud*, to lead them the way; and *by night in a pillar of fire*, to give them light.

Exodus 16:10 The glory of the Lord appeared in the *cloud*.

Exodus 19:9 And the Lord said unto Moses, Lo, I come unto thee in a thick *cloud*, that the people may hear when I speak with thee, and believe thee forever.

Exodus 24:18 And Moses went into the midst of the *cloud*.

Exodus 34:5 And the Lord descended in the *cloud*.

In light of *Bible* verses and other evidence for UFOs, God perhaps led the Israelites out of Egypt by day in a *cloud* (UFO) and by night in that same cloud "lit up as if with fire." If not, what was in the sky guiding the Israelites? *Bible* historians agree that the Exodus occurred between 1600 and 1200 BC when more than one hundred thousand Israelites fled Egypt after four-hundred years of slavery. A map of possible Exodus routes is provided below. The starting point was likely Succoth with the end point being Jebel Musa, where the tomb of Moses is believed to be located today.

Historians' Depiction of the Exodus Route

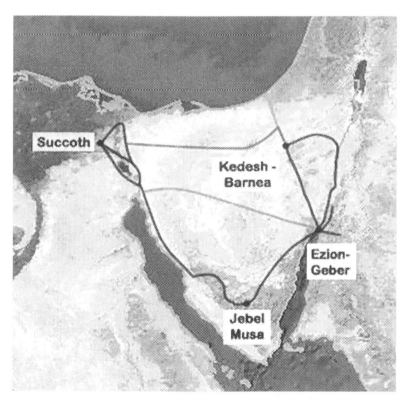

Source: *http://en.wikipedia.org/wiki/File:Exodus_Map.jpg*

The book of Ezekiel has more UFO eyewitness accounts than any other book of the *Bible*. Ezekiel saw a UFO hover, extend legs for landing, and then land, as noted in the following verses below. *Bible* historians also know that the Lord chose Ezekiel to try and reinstate his chosen people who had fallen under the covert control of the fallen angels and Satan.

Ezekiel 3:17 … I have made thee a watchman unto the house of Israel: therefore hear the word at my mouth, and give them warning from me.

Ezekiel 1:4-7 And I looked, and, behold, a *whirlwind* came out of the north, a great *cloud*, and a fire infolding itself, and a brightness was about it, and out of the midst thereof as the *colour of amber*, out of the midst of the fire. … *a huge cloud glowing with fire, with a mass of fire inside that flashed continually; and in the fire there was something that shone like polished brass.* Also out of the midst thereof came the likeness of four living creatures (landing pads). And this was their appearance; and every one had four wings. And their feet were straight feet; and the sole of their feet was like the sole of a calf's foot: and *they sparkled like the colour of burnished brass.*

Ezekiel 1:27 And I saw as the *colour of amber*, as the appearance of fire round about within it, from the appearance of his loins even upward, and from the appearance of his loins even downward, I saw as it were the appearance of fire, and *it had brightness round about.*

Like Ezekiel, the prophet Elijah (ascended) "went up into Heaven in a Whirlwind" at Beth-El. The ascent of Elijah was prearranged as God told him to go to Beth-El on a specific day. When Elijah arrived at Beth-El, a "chariot of fire, and horses of fire appeared and took him." Many reliable people saw Elijah ascend into a UFO at night.

UFOs have powerful weapons. For example, a beam of light from a cloud destroyed Sodom and Gomorrah and also destroyed the massive walls of Jericho. These powerful lasers (or some kind of weapon) were seen by thousands of people. Ancient civilizations across the planet passed down writings and stories of UFOs using powerful weapons. Consider the following *Bible* verses that record what some observers saw:

Joshua 6:20-21 … and the wall fell down flat, so that the people went up into the city, every man straight before him, and they took the city. And they utterly destroyed all that was in the city, both man and woman, young and old, and ox, and sheep, and ass, with the edge of the sword.

Genesis 19:24 Then the LORD rained upon Sodom and upon Gomorrah brimstone and fire.

2 Peter 2:6 And turning the cities of Sodom and Gomorrah into ashes condemned them with an overthrow, making them an example unto those that after should live ungodly.

Luke 17:29 But the same day that Lot went out of Sodom it rained fire and brimstone from heaven and destroyed them all.

Amos 2:12 But I will send a fire upon Moab, and it shall devour the palaces of Kerioth: and Moab shall die with tumult, with shouting, and with the sound of the trumpet.

Matthew 2:9 When they had heard the king, they departed; and, lo, the *star*, which they saw in the east, *went before them, til it came and stood* over where the young child was.

God the Father presumably guided the three wise men to the birthplace of Jesus. A simple star would not move like the wise men described nor hover like a UFO over the infant. The wise men were likely both wise and accurate in what they reported and described.

Moses ascended into a cloud (UFO) as indicated in the *Bible*, and Jacob witnessed angels going up a sky ladder into the clouds (UFO). The patriarch Jacob was spending the night in a field outside of Haran when he saw "angels of the Lord busily going up and down "a ladder set up on earth and its top reaching heavenwards." A depiction of the Jacob's Ladder event described in Genesis 28:10-22 is illustrated on the next page:

Jacob's Ladder As Described In (Genesis 28:10-22)

Source: *http://en.wikipedia.org/wiki/File:JacobsLaddertoHeaven.jpg*

In Ezekiel Chapter 28, the ruler of Tyre, a Phoenician city, ascended into a UFO. Jesus himself ascended into a cloud (UFO) (Acts 1:9). Harry Orlinsky says, "modern historians have come to accept much of the *Bible* as constituting unusually reliable historical documents of antiquity ..." Professor William Albright at Johns Hopkins University says: "The *Bible*'s languages, the life and customs of its peoples, its history, and its ethical and religious ideas are all illustrated in innumerable ways by archaeological discovery."

After the death and resurrection of Jesus, the presence of UFOs did not cease by any means. For example, in 312 AD, Constantine and his army saw UFOs and the craft aided them in fighting. In 329 AD, Constantine and his army saw two UFOs during their invasion of Asia. While crossing a river, Constantine and his men saw what was described as gleaming, silver shields in the sky. The objects repeatedly swooped down at opposing soldiers, scattering men and horses and creating a panic.

In 336 AD, while attacking a Venetian city in the eastern Mediterranean, observers on both sides of the conflict reported another incredible event. UFOs appeared in the sky and shot a beam of light at the city wall, crumbling it to dust. This allowed Constantine to easily take the city. It is widely believed that Constantine seeing a UFO spawned the whole Roman Empire converting to Christianity. In 776 AD, Charlemagne's castle at Sigiburg was attacked by the Saxons and suddenly two UFOs appeared and killed the attacking Saxons. These events are well documented in history.

In summary, the UFO-*Bible* connection is quite clear. The Vatican acknowledges the likelihood of UFOs; close to one thousand *Bible* verses arguably report UFO sightings. The overall evidence indicates that God the Father may have been onsite in a UFO, directing the wise men, the Exodus, the resurrection, the parting of the Red Sea, the Flood, and other events described in the *Bible*. More than two thirds of the books in the *Bible* contain some kind of reference to unidentified flying objects. UFOs are not synonymous with Satan or demons and witnesses to these craft are not "possessed" or part of a cult. That mentality of the Dark Ages is clearly inappropriate today. Let's now examine evidence from other sources before reaching conclusions regarding the UFO-Christianity connection.

Chapter 3:
THE UFO-ENOCH CONNECTION

There are two Enochs in the *Bible*. The first was born in 4784 BC and was the son of Cain who was born in 4969 BC. This first Enoch is not that important for our purpose here except for the fact that his father named a city after him. The more important Enoch in ancient history was born in 3238 BC. He was an important prophet mentioned in *Bible* verses such as 1 Chronicales 1:3, Luke 3:37, and Hebrews 11:5. The prophet Enoch was the great-grandfather of Noah and the father of Methuselah (Genesis 5:1-18). Enoch's temple was built in Canaan which eventually became Israel. In the *Quran*, the prophet Enoch is referred to as Idrees in Surah Al-Anbiya (the prophets) verse 85 and in Surah Maryam (Mary) verse 56.

Enoch was of such great righteousness that God saved him from death. Hebrews 11:5 says, "By faith Enoch was translated that he should not see death; and he was not found, because God translated him: for he hath had witness borne to him that before his translation he had been well pleasing unto God." What is most interesting about the prophet Enoch is that he spent sixty days traveling aboard a UFO with archangel Uriel as his guide. Uriel showed Enoch the underworld and explained the nature of truth and reality to Enoch. Then God gave Enoch thirty days to return to earth and tell mankind about Satan, the underworld, and salvation. The seventh from Adam (Jude 1: 14-15),

Enoch then prophesized to ungodly men that God shall come with His holy ones to judge and convict them.

Enoch witnessed God's "chariots" as indicated in these verses: Enoch 24:1-4 He (Enoch) mounted a cherub and flew. He (God) has the *chariots* of wind, as it is written, He soared on the wings of the wind. He has the *chariots* of swift cloud, as it is written. See! The Lord comes riding a swift cloud. He has the *chariots* of clouds, as it is written, "I am coming to you in a dense cloud." Enoch 24:6 says, "He has the chariots of twice ten thousand, as it is written, The chariots of God are twice ten thousand, thousands of angels."

Enoch also witnessed Elijah ascending up into a "whirlwind." Enoch 2:1 says, "And it came to pass, when the LORD would take up Elijah into heaven by a whirlwind, that Elijah went with Elisha from Gilgal." Enoch 2:11 states, "And it came to pass, as they still walked on, and talked, that, behold, there appeared a chariot of fire, and horses of fire, and parted them both asunder; and Elijah went up by a whirlwind into heaven."

Written around 200 BC by one or more authors, the *Book of Enoch* is one of the earliest texts known to mankind. Jude 14:15 quotes from the first chapter of the *Book of Enoch*. The *Book of Enoch* was not included in the canon of Scripture, but the Ethiopian Christian Church has long accepted the *Book of Enoch* as principle and as part of the Apocrypha. The *Book of Enoch* was often referenced among early theologians. Many early church fathers approved and supported the Enochian writings, including Justin Martyr (100-165), Tatian (110-172), Ienaeus, Clement of Alexandria (150-220), Tertullian (160-230), Origen (186-255), Lactantius (260-330), as well as Methodius of Philippi, Minucius Felix, Commodianus, and Ambrose of Milan.

The *Book of Enoch* disappeared sometime after the fall of the Roman Empire about 800 AD but was rediscovered in 1773 in Abyssinia, Ethiopia by famous explorer James Bruce. About 1128 AD, after the First Crusade, The Knights Templar, descendants of the Jerusalem priesthood, dug deep below Soloman's Temple and supposedly found Enoch's lost secrets and instantly became the richest and most influential religious order the world has ever known. This document is one of the earliest texts known to mankind. Enoch was supposedly 365 years old when he ascended into a UFO. The *Jewish Encyclopedia* says the *Book of Enoch* is one of the most important pieces of apocalyptic literature and is a valuable source of information about the Messiah.

The *Book of Enoch* explains how the sons of God, called "watchers," long ago were some of God's angels whom God entrusted to watch over and care for people, but their lust for women led them to rebel along with Satan. The *Book of Enoch* clearly says "watchers" took daughters of men as wives who gave birth to giants (discussed in Chapter 12) who eventually became very evil and consumed all the acquisitions of men. The *Book of Enoch* calls the watchers "fallen angels" and "Nephilim" because they came to be despised by God.

The term "watchers" is mentioned twice in the Old Testament, once in the *Book of Job* and three times in Daniel. Without God's permission, watchers taught mankind about astronomy, metallurgy, mathematics, cosmetics, jewelry, medical, and the art of war as well as the methods of writing. Enoch 8:1-2 says, "And Azaz'el taught the people the art of making swords and knives, and shields, and breastplates; and he showed to their chosen ones bracelets, decorations, eye shadowing, ornamentation, all kinds of precious stones, and all coloring tinctures and alchemy. And there were many wicked ones and they committed adultery and erred, and all their conduct became corrupt."

God showed Enoch the underworld of the earth where demons and Satan perhaps reside. Enoch 21: 3 says, "I exclaimed, for what specific crime have they been bound, and why have they been removed to this place? (the underworld) Then Uriel, one of the holy angels who was with me, and who conducted me, answered: Enoch, wherefore dost thou ask; wherefore reason with thyself, and anxiously inquired? These are those of the stars which have transgressed the commandment of the most high God; and are here bound, until the infinite number of the days of their crimes be completed."

The *Book of Enoch* is especially important because it reveals Enoch's knowledge while traveling with the angel Uriel in a UFO. The UFO-

Enoch connection is quite clear. If God and angels used UFOs in various events described in the *Bible*, and if the Enoch story is true, then perhaps God's watchers use these craft even today to carry out his will on earth. Let's now examine the writings from several ancient civilizations to determine possible UFO connections there, before deciding whether the UFO-Christianity connection is true or false.

Chapter 4:
THE UFO-EGYPT CONNECTION

Most of the pyramids in Egypt were built beginning around 3100 BC. However, many scholars believe the Great Pyramid of Giza could not have been built by the Egyptians - at least not without ancient alien help. The earliest Egyptian writings say the pyramids were originally built "to store knowledge" rather than "as tombs for pharoahs." Known as "The Sleeping Prophet," Edgar Cayce and researcher Kurt Mendelssohn among others believed the Great Pyramid of Giza was built as a cooperative effort between Egyptian residents as laborers and Atlantean (from Atlantis – discussed in Chapter 10) architects. A picture of the Great Pyramid of Giza is given on the next page.

Like many other megalithic structures worldwide, evidence suggests that the Pyramid of Giza may have served as a navigation marker for UFOs. Listed below are several reasons why the Great Pyramid of Giza was *not* built by the Egyptians, at least not without high-tech help from somebody or something:

1. No humans around 3100 BC knew the exact center of the earth, which is the precise center of the Pyramid of Giza within several inches.
2. No humans at that time knew exact north vs south vs east vs west, which is the exact layout of the Pyramid of Giza, being off only 3/60th of a degree.

3. No humans at that time knew the exact curvature of the earth, which is the exact
curvature of the sides of the Pyramid, identically mirroring latitude/longitude lines today.
4. No humans then or now could cut, polish, and stack more than a million blocks averaging 2.5 million tons each to thousandths of an inch tolerance, which is what was used to build the Pyramid of Giza.
5. No humans back then could square all two hundred-plus levels of the Pyramid of Giza to within less than an inch.
6. No humans back then could transport the millions of blocks over land distances nor float them across the Nile River. Maybe the blocks were "air lifted" because the quarry for the stones is miles away across the river.
7. No humans back then - or even today - could cut shafts (a hole) in each stone so that when placed on top of each other all the holes are aligned to the star Sirius and the constellation Orion. Researcher Robert Devall first confirmed these alignments.
8. The Pyramid of Giza rises at a tricky, steep, fifty-two degree angle, but most (if not all) other pyramids in Egypt and around the world rise at precisely a 43.5-degree angle. This latter fact could not be a mere coincidence.

The Great Pyramid of Giza

Source: *http://en.wikipedia.org/wiki/File:Kheops-Pyramid.jpg*

The Great Pyramid of Giza was likely built thousands of years before 3100 BC. At 455 feet in height and with highly reflective surfaces, for a thousand years or more the Pyramid at Giza could be seen from far away in outer space. It was the tallest structure in the world until the Empire State Building was built in New York City. The Second Pyramid at Giza is shorter than the Great Pyramid, but their peaks are at the exact same height above sea level. Ancient aliens likely used the Pyramid of Giza, as well as other pyramids across the planet, as a navigation tool.

The Great Sphinx at Giza pictured below is located next to the Great Pyramid but is much older. The Sphinx shows signs of extensive water erosion, which some scholars believe indicates it was there before the flood (discussed in chapter 11). Regardless of who originally built the Great Sphinx, it was modified several times, including by Pharaoh Khafre in the Sixth Dynasty, whose face was likely sculptured to replace a lion's face.

The Great Sphinx at Giza

Source: *http://en.wikipedia.org/wiki/File:Great_Sphinx_of_Giza_-_20080716a.jpg*

Astrophysicist Thomas Brody says the layout of the megalithic stone site near Giza at Nabta in Egypt may date to 16,500 BC and is also an astronomical masterpiece aligned to the star Sirius and the constellation Orion. Also around 16,500 BC, there were very advanced astronomic observatories in the Sahara. Traditional archaeologists and anthropologists however maintain that prehistoric man was extremely backward at 16,500 BC, surviving only with spears and stone tools. More and more archaeological evidence uncovered everyday however refutes this contention.

On May 23, 2010, Egypt's Supreme Council of Antiquities reported unearthing fifty-seven ancient Egyptian tombs, most of which held an ornately painted wooden sarcophagus with a mummy inside. The oldest tombs date back to around 2750 BC during the period of Egypt's first and second dynasties. Twelve of the tombs belong to the eighteenth dynasty which ruled Egypt during the second millennium BC. Abdel Rahman El-Aydi, head of the archaeological mission that made the discovery, said some of the tombs are decorated with religious texts that ancient Egyptians believed would help the deceased cross through to the underworld. The underworld (discussed in chapter 14) is the domain of Satan, so most likely the Egyptians were worshiping fallen angels.

NASA's Viking photographs of Mars show a five-sided pyramid and several four-sided pyramids. Richard Hoagland, who received the 1997 Ig Nobel Award for Astronomy, says he obtained the photographs and released them but NASA has not acknowledged the photos are of pyramids. NASA did acknowledge in 2002 that its *Odyssey* spacecraft found lots of ice below the surface of Mars. In January 1985, NASA discovered what is called the Venus Complex on Venus. Pyramids on Venus are also sometimes referred to as the Cytherean Complex which reportedly includes a Sphinx identical to one at Giza. If there are pyramids on Mars and/or Venus as some persons claim, then UFOs clearly visited those planets too.

On balance, the UFO-Egypt connection is quite clear because there is just no way people at 3100 BC or even today could build the Great Pyramid of Giza without very heavy equipment (or gravity-defying forces) to cut, transport, and stack millions of multi-ton stones to perfection. The Egyptians' continual reference to the underworld implies that they may have received assistance from fallen angels. But let's examine other civilizations and other topics regarding possible UFO connections before drawing conclusions as to whether the UFO-Christianity link is strong or weak.

Chapter 5:
THE UFO-SUMERIAN CONNECTION

Traditional science says everything advanced about mankind began with the Sumerian (or Sumer) civilization that rose around 3800 BC (perhaps earlier) in Mesopotamia – between the Tigris and Euphrates Rivers in present-day Iraq. The Sumerians were the first people to have cities with grid streets, sewer systems, and writing systems. Prior to the Sumerians, nothing was written down. Civilizations before 3800 BC simply used pictures, carvings, and stories to pass down information to future generations. The first writings were pictographs carved in clay in vertical columns, and later turned horizontal, and then later in Sumer became cuneiform writing. The earliest form of paper, papyrus was first used about 3800 BC and represented a major advance over writing on clay tablets. A map of ancient Sumer is given on the next page. Note the location of the cities to be mentioned later: Nippur, Kish, Eridu, Jericho, Tyre, and Ur. Note the area between the Tigris and Euphrates Rivers that extend westward from the Persian Gulf through Mesopotamia. The bold line indicates the major trade route of that time.

Fred R. David, PhD

An Ancient Map of Sumeria

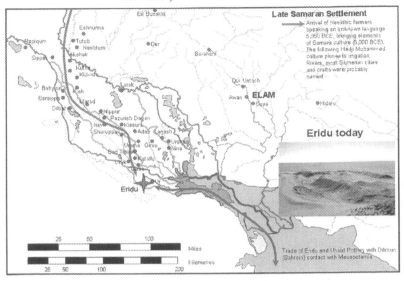

Source: *http://en.wikipedia.org/wiki/File:Sumer1.jpg*

Called the Pentateuch, the first five books of the *Bible* were written about 1260 BC by Moses, according to Jewish history. However, the Sumerian writings were much earlier and included much of what is in the Pentateuch. In 3760 BC, the Sumerians established mankind's first calendar, the Calendar of Nippur. This calendar is still in use today as the Jewish religious calendar. Our year 2012 will be year 5772 on the Calendar of Nippur.

Historians do not understand how or even why prehistoric man making primitive tools for over a hundred thousand years all of the sudden around 3800 BC became metallurgists, astronomers, mathematicians, musicians, physicists, doctors, writers, and farmers. Why did the sudden advancement happen at all? The *Book of Enoch* and other writings say fallen angels taught man science. The Sumerians say, "Whatever seems beautiful, we made by the grace of the gods." The Sumerians acknowledge having help from the watchers, i.e.. fallen angels, whom they thought were gods. The Sumerians repeatedly proclaimed in both pictures and writings that extraterrestrials in UFOs, called shems, were their gods and governed them. Sumerian gods, they said, came from the star system Pleiades, commonly called the Seven Sisters, in the constellation Taurus.

Sumerian gods were like the Greek gods, described as physically similar to men and women and human in character. They could be happy or sad or mad and they were visible, physical beings that had offspring with human women. This description is quite similar to the biblical God. Sumerian gods could travel at immense speeds, appear, disappear, and had powerful laser-like weapons. The Greek's primary god was Zeus whose chief weapon was the thunderbolt and who resided in the sky. The most powerful Sumerian god was Anu who they called the Great Father or the King of the Gods. Their second most powerful was Enlil. The city of Nippur, seen on the Sumeria map, was dedicated to Enlil. Although a god, Enlil was also human. The third great god of Sumeria was another son of Anu, named Enki. Like the *Bible*, the Sumerian civilization believed that god created man in a conscious act.

The capital of Sumeria was initially Kish, then Uruk, but their religious center was always Nippur, located one hundred miles south of present-day Baghdad. According to Sumerian writings, Anu stayed in a UFO and rarely descended to earth, so his first son, Enlil, managed all gods and men in Sumer. Enlil arrived on earth long before man was civilized. A reasonable conclusion from ancient writings is that fallen angels had and have UFOs, God and his true angels had and have UFOs, and Satan had and has UFOs. Before the flood, Nippur was mission control center for Enlil's command and communication center on earth. After the flood, the control center shifted to Jerusalem.

The Sumerians erected a shem or launch tower or sky vehicle, in the city of Babel. Perhaps this was the Tower of Babel mentioned in Genesis, Chapter 11. The Sumerians did not want to lose track of one another as man spread all over Eurasia, so they wanted a shem. This tower however made God very mad and he supposedly changed the language of people due to this tower. Ancient writings indicate the Tower of Babel was built in 3450 BC.

Sumerian writings report that several men were chosen to ascend into a UFO, including Adapa. Another was Gilgamesh, who like Enoch came back to earth after spending time with god. One of the oldest written texts developed by the Sumerians was the *Epic of Gilgamesh* which speaks of the ruler Uruk who was born to a mortal father and a divine mother and was said to be two-thirds god and one-third human. Virtually every story in Genesis is mentioned in the Sumerian writings.

Sumerian writings say that God (called Anunnaki, Enki, Nefilim, or Yahew) arrived on earth in 442,000 BC in need of gold and water. Soon thereafter, their writings say the gods purposefully altered prehistoric man to create slave workers for mining operations. Sumerians recorded that "gods" came to earth to mine gold. Gold is essential for electricity, it reflects infrared light, and it is an excellent heat shield, perhaps the best. The only metal that really lasts is gold; it is indestructible. Aliens supposedly sent expeditions here to obtain gold, but mining is tough work, so they needed slaves. At the Web site *http://www.viewzone2.com/adamscalendarx.html,* explorers such as Cyril Hromnik, Richard Wade, and Johan Heine assert that various stone structures in South Africa are two hundred thousand years old and are the remains of temples and astronomical observatories of lost ancient civilizations engaged in extensive gold mining.

Prehistoric mining operations dating back one hundred thousand years or more have been discovered at numerous sites around the world, including at Lion Cavern, near Ngwenya in Swaziland, South Africa, and at Border Cave in South Africa, and on Keweenaw Peninsula in North America, and on Isle Royale near the northern shore of Lake Superior in Michigan, and the Lion Coal Mine in Wattis, Utah, as well as in Peru. Evidence at all ancient mining sites shows that thousands of tons of excavated ore were transported thousands of miles away by some unknown means. In addition to gold, mining operations were also aimed at obtaining hematite, often called "bloodstone" because it is used as a cosmetic and as a substitute for human blood in ritual ceremonies.

Also according to Sumerian writings, gods created giants by altering the human DNA code. Adam and Eve may have been the first genetically achieved slave people. Adam is who the Sumerians say was the first slave man. Sumerian writings say aliens began mining in South Africa back one hundred fifty thousand years. Various tribes in Africa even today assert that aliens visited them thousands of years ago, including the Zulu, who assert that aliens came for mining over one million years ago.

Sumerian archeological sites today are covered with clay figurines that depict extraterrestrial-looking people with "goggles" as eyes and often with helmets. Scores of these figurines were found for example at Tell Brak, a prehistoric site on the Khabur River. This is the same river where Ezekiel saw a divine chariot. An early Sumerian ruler named Enmedurannki was invited to ascend into a cloud (UFO) and he did so.

Ancient Sumerian tablets corroborate the *Bible*, archeological findings, and the *Book of Enoch* that say mankind learned how to make beautiful clothes, weapons of war, complex metals, etc. from arrival on earth of aliens (gods/fallen angels/extraterrestrials, ancient astronauts are analogous terms). The Sumerian annals indicate that their alien teachers were luminous beings that navigated through the sky in disc-shaped craft of fire. The *Bible* too refers to luminous beings, including Jesus and angels. The Sumerians named one fallen angel Azazel, a name often used for Satan.

The Sumerians believed there were twelve gods. Nippur was the Sumerian religious center and prized city of the gods. Some scholars believe that as far back as 360,000 BC, Bad-tibira, the Sumerian city in southern Iraq, was God's metallurgical center for smelting and refining. Bad-tibira was the second city in Sumeria to "exercise kingship," following the city of Eridu. At the Web site *http://www.youtube.com/watch?v=3lGN5iq9azU&NR=1*, Dr. Michael Zimmerman provides a ten-minute documentary on Sumerian gods and evidence for ancient alien visitation on earth. He talks about how gods genetically engineered man for the purpose of being primitive workers.

35

Sumerian writings say God allowed lower-level gods to breed with prehistoric man (perhaps Neanderthals who lived from 1 million BC to 25,000 BC) to genetically produce primitive workers for use as slaves that worked even while naked. Prehistoric man was not "engineered to worship god" but rather was "engineered to be slave workers." However by about 100,000 BC, the Sumerian writings say the sons of lower-level gods took the daughters of man as wives and this infuriated God and eventually led God to allow the Great Flood. Genesis 6 says, "When the Earthlings began to increase in number upon the face of the Earth, and daughters were born unto them, that the sons of the deities saw the daughters of the Earthlings that they were compatible, and they took unto themselves wives of whichever they chose. And the deity said, "my spirit shall not shield man forever; having strayed, he is but flesh." A commonly accepted depiction of what a Neanderthal man probably looked like is given below, followed by a skull comparison illustration on the next page.

Common Depiction of a Neanderthal Male's Profile

Source: http://en.wikipedia.org/wiki/File:Neanderthaler_Fund.png

Comparing a Neanderthal Skull (Right Column)
With a Human Skull Today (Left Column)

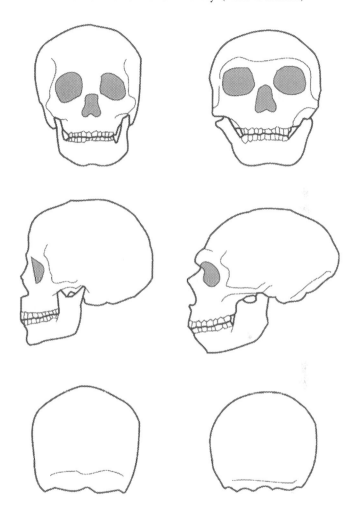

Source: http://en.wikipedia.org/wiki/File:Neandertal_vs_Sapiens.jpg

Bjorn Kurten, author of *Not from the Apes* says, "It has been possible in the last decade to demonstrate that the human lineage can be followed back into far more distant times where it still retains its unique character. Indeed, we may doubt that our ancestor was ever what could properly be called an ape. This makes excellent sense zoologically. The contrasts between apes and men in anatomy are too great to be reconciled with a relatively recent common origin, and the same is true of behavior." (pp. 4-5, 1972, *Pantheon Books,* 1972).

On May 7, 2010, Harvard geneticist David Reich in *Science* announced that Neanderthal men and women did in fact interbreed with Cro-Magnon man because he discovered uniquely Neanderthal DNA in our present-day DNA. In the July 8, 2010 edition of *Nature,* scientists reported discovering that Neanderthals, much like modern- day people, carved out a living at a spot on the east coast of England roughly nine hundred thousand years ago, when the area would have resembled today's southern Scandinavia in climate and landscape. Never before had early humans been shown to live so far north so far back in time. Anthropologists every year back up the date in time when humans first lived on earth.

Neanderthal and Cro-Magnon man did not suddenly become mathematicians, metallurgists, physicists, and astronomers. The two groups overlapped from about 35,000 BC to 25,000 BC until Neanderthal became extinct. Ancient texts from across the planet describe and portray beings that "came from the sky and gave them knowledge." Writings, pictures, and carvings of gods descending from the sky and ascending into a cloud are common among virtually all religions of the world. The collaborative evidence for UFOs from so many ancient civilizations is increasingly being taken seriously rather than ignored.

On balance, the UFO-Sumerian connection is exceptionally strong. Early Sumerian writings left no doubt that gods traveling in UFOs greatly impacted not only their civilization but also the evolution of mankind more than a hundred thousand years ago. Much of the Sumerian writings found their way into the Old Testament. Based on Sumerian writings, it appears perhaps that fallen angels (aliens) came to earth, impregnated Neanderthal women, and forced the human species into an evolutionary leap. Genesis 6:2 says, "That the sons of God saw the daughters of men that they were fair; and they took them wives of all which they chose. Many *Bible* verses refer to the "sons of gods" (discussed in chapter 13) such as the twenty-ninth Psalm. The Sumerians may have been worshiping Satan and fallen angels. This would be an easy mistake to make because (1) Satan and his forces in the underworld have godlike powers, and (2) Jesus was still three thousand years away. Before addressing the UFO-Christianity relationship, let's examine the UFO connection with other ancient civilizations.

Chapter 6:
THE UFO-INCA CONNECTION

Historians date the Inca Empire to the period 1100 AD to 1532 AD, but actually Inca history may go back thousands of years before that time. The Inca's originally settled near Lake Titicaca in southern Peru. This area was the metallurgical capital of the Americas for hundreds if not thousands of years, having tons of gold, silver, copper, and tin available in surrounding mountains. The Inca Empire at its height extended along the South American Pacific Coast and Andes Mountains from Ecuador to the Maule River in central Chile, but their primary country was Peru.

In 1532 when Spanish explorer Francisco Pizarro and 180 soldiers landed on the coast of Peru, the Incas thought he was their creator god, Viracocha. The soldiers had cannons, which confirmed for the Incas that Pizarro was Viracocha, a god who controlled the sound of thunder. The Incas at the time literally had tons of gold, a vast road system, highly developed irrigation systems, palaces, temples, and fortifications. The Inca emperor Atahualpa and his people saw the magical technology of Pizarro's forces and were sure the Spaniards were descendants of the great Viracocha. This mistake enabled the Spanish to kidnap and execute Atahualpa, loot the Inca temples of their gold, demonize their religion, and effectively dismantle their empire – identical to what Cortez did to the Aztecs eleven years earlier.

At an altitude of 11,200 feet, Cuzco in Peru is the famous Inca capital city, known for its astounding megalithic stones weighing upwards of twenty-five tons each and cut and carved to precision similar to the Pyramid of Giza stones. The Cuzco stones were transported there from many miles away, cut to fit odd angles perfectly, then raised and placed atop each other, and then held tightly together without mortar. The Inca believed the Cuzco structures were built by aliens with UFOs or built by giants. The Inca readily acknowledged they inherited the structures rather than building them.

In both Cuzco and Giza as well as other places around the earth, megalithic stones fifteen to twenty feet wide and high weighing fifteen to two hundred tons apiece were moved, shaped, lifted, engraved, and handled with ease more than a thousand years before Christ. It is unlikely that primitive man could do that unassisted. Recall that most American Indians in the mid-1800s were still using bows and arrows to kill game. All over the planet, the older the pyramids or structures, the more sophisticated their astronomical and mathematical precision. That is counter-intuitive but an accepted fact. Archeologists such as Maria Schulten say the megalithic structures in South and Central America were built about 3172 BC.

In addition to Cuzco, there are pre-Inca megalithic structures in Peru at Machu Picchu where Viracocha's tomb is located, and at Ollantaytambu (40 miles north of Cuzco), and Sacsahuaman. These sites as well as Tiahuanacu all lie on an exact 45-degree line starting at the Island of the Sun in Lake Titicaca. At an elevation of 13,861 feet, during the Inca days, Tiahuanacu during the Inca days was located on the southernmost tip of Lake Titicaca. Since then the lake has receded, so that today, Tiahuanacu is located twelve miles south of the southernmost tip of the lake. The Island of the Sun (actually Island of Titicaca) and the Island of the Moon (actually Coati) are near Tiahuanacu, which was the Inca capital before Cuzco. At the Web site *http://www.youtube.com/watch?v =P2YBVlgqqco&NR=1&feature=fvwp*, Michael Palin provides a three-minute narrated tour of Machu Picchu and the Inca civilization. Several pictures of Cuzco as the city appears today is given on the next page.

The City of Cuzco, Peru As It Looks Today

Source: *http://en.wikipedia.org/wiki/File:Cuscoinfobox.png*

Comprising 3,210 square miles, Lake Titicaca is the second largest lake in South America and the highest navigable lake in the world. At 12,500 feet in elevation, Lake Titicaca is also deep, reaching 1,000 feet in depth. This body of water may be an entry point into the underworld. Lake Titicaca is where the Inca god Viracocha performed his creative feats and is where mankind supposedly reappeared after the flood. Viracocha may have been a survivor from Atlantis. Ephraim George Squier was convinced that the Titicaca area stones, carvings, and statues were the work of giants. Near Titicaca are two of the highest peaks in the Americas, perhaps the highest and very similar to twin peaks of Ararat (17,000 and 13,000 feet) in the Middle East. A three-minute narrated tour of Lake Titicaca is provided at the Web site *http://www.youtube.com/watch?v=lAQhpwoH3c8,* including coverage of the Inca living at Lake Titicaca today. A map of the lake is given below:

A Map of Lake Titicaca

Source: *http://en.wikipedia.org/wiki/File:Lake_Titicaca_map.png*

Dating back perhaps to 16,500 BC, the ruins of Tiahuanacu, originally named Taypicala, as well as the ruins at Puma Punku (one mile from Tiahuanacu) in the Bolivian Andes, feature a very highly advanced civilization of skilled metallurgists and astronomers. It is possible that fallen angels or aliens of some kind impacted this area with their UFOs and/or their offspring - giants. At Puma Punku for example, two-hundred-plus ton cut and polished stones are made out of dyrite and granite, two of the hardest stones. In fact, dyrite is the hardest stone except for diamond. That means diamond-edged or tipped cutting machines of immense size had to have etched in the grooves and designs in the Puma Punku stones, unbelievable for primitive man without ancient alien assistance. And the quarry for the Puma Punku stones was ten miles away on the western shore of Lake Titicaca. One stone at Puma Punku weighs close to four hundred tons and it too was moved, etched, and stacked.

Many of the stones at Puma Punku have large metal clamps that hold some blocks together. Analyses performed with an electron microscope have determined that these clamps are comprised of a copper-nickel alloy and poured into the shaped-slots already carved into the rock. The technology to produce this alloy would require a smelter that could reach a temperature of 3,500 degrees. Such technology became available only in 1930 AD (not) BC. The Puma Punka stones are one of only three places in the ancient world to use metal I-clamps to join cut blocks. The other two places are ancient Egypt and Angkor Wat in Cambodia.

Arthur Posnansky, a European engineer who moved to Bolivia and devoted his lifetime to studying artifacts at Titicaca, discovered that bronze clamps held many of the ancient boulders together. Bronze also is a very difficult alloy to produce being a mixture of copper and tin. Working with architect Edmund Kiss, Posnansky determined that the astronomical alignments of the Kalasasaya Pyramid at Titicaca and its interior stairways suggested that the structures were built circa 15,000 BC. He and many other scientists knew this because the tilt of the earth's axis changes slightly yearly, and the Kalasasaya cornerstones and gateways aligned to the year 15,000 BC. Some of the huge stone statues at Tiahaunaco look identical to those on Easter Island in the South Pacific. There are also sculptures in some of the temples at Tiahuanaco that resemble elephants. However elephants have not lived in North or South America since around 10,900 BC as evidenced in the geologic record.

Posnansky believed Tiahuanacu was the oldest city in the world, one that was "built before the flood." The German Astronomical Commission sent an expedition to Peru and Bolivia to check out Posnansky's findings. Headed by Professor (Dr.) Arnold Kohlschutter, director of the Astronomical Observatory in Bonn and the honorary astronomer of the Vatican, and Dr. Rolf Muller, astronomer from the Potsdam Observatory, these scientists agreed with Posnansky regarding 15,000 BC but said an alternative period of time would have been 9,300 BC for the Titicaca ruins. Some of the stones in the Kalasasaya temple weigh 120 tons. Posnansky's findings were later corroborated by Dr. Hans Ludendorff, Dr. Arnold Kohlschutter, and Dr. Rolf Muller. Some kind of super race of beings with UFO type knowledge and power probably also built the gigantic astronomical structures in Tiahuanacu, Cuzco, Puma Punka, Ollantaytambo, and Sacsayhuaman.

Also in Inca country, the Nazca Drawings in Peru can be viewed only from the air between the towns of Nazca and Palpa. On the Peruvian coast below Lima, the Nazca region is a large flat plain on a mountain. An entire mountaintop has been removed by some kind of very heavy sophisticated machinery. The whole area once upon a time was a gigantic mining operation, perhaps a hundred thousand years ago. Traditional science says gigantic bulldozers and saws became available only in the twentieth century AD, contrary to the evidence at many locations worldwide.

There are abundant raw materials at Nazca and there are perfectly straight lines reminiscent of runways, as well as huge geometric and animal designs. There is a gigantic spider, a one-thousand-foot-long pelican, a hummingbird, a snake, and a lama. The gigantic, elaborate designs drawn on the ground can be seen only from the sky. Evidence suggests the lines were some kind of communication system with UFOs more than a thousand years ago. Researchers Paul Koosk and Dr. Maria Reiche, famous astronomers and mathematicians, studied the Nazca Drawings and concluded the Nazca Lines represented a great astronomical observatory that predicted the future locations of stars, planets, the sun, and the moon. A picture taken from an airplane of a Nazca Drawing is given on the next page:

A Nazca Drawing of a Monkey

Source: *http://en.wikipedia.org/wiki/File:Nazca_monkey.jpg*

The Incas believed there were five ages. The first was that of Viracochas, gods who were white and bearded. The second was that of the giants. The third was the age of primitive man. The fourth was the age of demigods (hybrid human animals). The fifth was the age of the Incas and of mankind today. All the South and Central American natives worshiped twelve gods, as did the ancient Sumerians, Greeks, Phoenicians, Hittites, Canaanites, and Babylonians. The Incas credit their god Viracocha for the creation of humankind as well as for the destruction of the worlds that preceded them and for the creation of new worlds. It is amazing how similar Inca beliefs were to biblical beliefs even though the Incas were thousands of miles and oceans away from the Middle East.

One of the Inca ages ended in 73,000 BC when the Toba volcanic eruption on the island of Sumatra in Indonesia blocked out sunlight on the earth for six years and dropped global temperatures twenty-eight degrees, plunging the earth into a deep ice age that lasted eighteen hundred years. This super-eruption on Sumatra nearly wiped out the human species leaving a very small gene pool from which all people today are descendants. The archaeological expeditions led by anthropologist Stanley Ambrose at the University of Illinois published these findings in the journal *Palaeogeography, Palaeoclimatology, Palaeoecology.* A similar super-eruption is expected to some day occur in Yellowstone National Park, coating most of the USA in a layer of ash three feet deep. A similar cataclysm occurred in 65,000,000 BC when a huge asteroid hit the Yucutan Peninsula creating the Chicxulub Crater in Mexico. Impact ash thrown into the atmosphere on that day blocked out the sun also for years, killing most plant life on the earth and all large dinosaurs.

The UFO-Inca connection is quite strong because there is just no way the Incas or their ancestors could have cut, moved, polished, carved, engraved, and then raised one-hundred-ton dyrite stones to build pyramids and structures aligned perfectly with the stars. The gigantic Nazca drawings can be seen only from the air, and UFOs were the only possible aerial vehicles a thousand years ago. Orville and Wilbur Wright are generally credited with flying the first airplane on December 17, 1903. The Inca people must have had some kind of fallen angel or alien assistance in the form of massive equipment or gravity-defying technology similar to what apparently is used for UFO propulsion. Let's examine the Aztec civilization next to determine whether a UFO connection exists there.

Chapter 7:
THE UFO-AZTEC CONNECTION

The Aztecs ruled central Mexico from 1300 AD to 1521 AD when Spanish explorer Hernan Cortes arrived on the coast. The Aztecs thought for sure Cortes was their main god, Quetzalcoatl. Both Quetzalcoatl, called the Feathered Serpent, and later Cortes arrived first near the city of Veracruz. Possibly a survivor from Atlantis or a fallen angel, Quetzalcoatl taught the Aztecs everything about the arts, architecture, astronomy, road building, and more. He was a white man with long dark hair and a flowing beard, and with his helpers, he civilized the whole Aztec nation.

Quetzalcoatl forbade all that was wrong including the sacrifice of human beings and animals, wars, fighting, robbery, and all violence. He came from the east and said he would someday return from the east with others like him. Mistaking Cortes for Quetzalcoatl "returning" allowed Cortes and his five hundred conquistadores with thirteen horses and a few small cannons to subdue an empire of millions.

Before the Aztecs, the Olmec civilization arose along the Mexican gulf coast around 2000 BC and was one of the oldest in the Americas. By 1200 BC, the Olmec civilization consisted of forty-plus cities. Pictured on a map in a moment, the Olmecs in the Americas were the first to have a calendar, art, jade, mathematics, metallurgy, celestial orientations, and more. The Olmecs, who may have been ancestors to the Maya as well, are compared to the Sumerians. Though thousands of miles apart, both civilizations described their phenomenal achievements as a "gift from the gods." Both civilizations referred often to "visitors to earth who could roam the skies" and "winged beings" who brought them knowledge. Whether they were speaking about fallen angels or Atlantis survivors or ancient aliens is not clear, but somebody or something with UFOs assisted the Olmecs. A map of Mexico and Central America is provided below to show where the Olmec Empire was located in 600 BC.

Located in Cholula, Mexico, the Great Pyramid of Cholula is the largest pyramid in the world by volume, even larger than the Great Pyramid of Giza, although not as tall. With a base of 450 by 450 meters and a height of 217 feet, Cholula was supposedly built by the Olmecs and then added on by the Toltecs and Aztecs. It was an astonishing astronomical observatory. The Aztecs believed the Cholula pyramid was built by giants, led by Xelhua, one of the seven giants in Aztec mythology who escaped the flood by ascending the mountain of Tialoc. The Aztecs dedicated the Cholula pyramid to their deity Quetzalcoatl.

The Olmec Empire in 600 BC

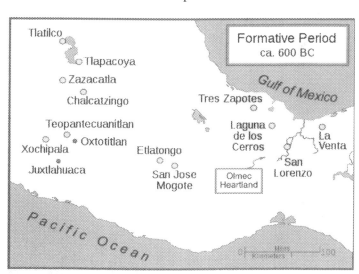

Source: *http://en.wikipedia.org/wiki/File:Formative_Era_sites.svg*

The Aztec capital was Tenochtitlan, also called the City of Tenoch, naming it after their ancestor, which might have been Enoch – yes, the same prophet discussed earlier. Since the Aztecs prefixed many of their words with the sound "T," Tenoch could have originally been Enoch. Tenochtitlan was located on an island in Lake Texcoco. Founded in 1325 AD, Tenochtitlan became the center of the Aztec Empire in the fifteenth century, until captured by Cortez in 1521. The ruins of Tenochtitlan are today located in the center of Mexico City.

Another ancient city in Mexico is Teotihuacan, located about twenty-five miles northeast of Mexico City. The ancient people of Teotihuacan worshiped many gods, including Quetzalcoatl. Religious leaders were the political leaders. Teotihuacanos practiced human sacrifice, since executed victims' skeletons have been found during excavations of the pyramids at Teotihuacan, also known for its large residential complexes, the Avenue of the Dead, and numerous colorful, well-preserved murals. The city was founded around 200 BC, lasting until its fall sometime between the seventh and eighth centuries AD. At its zenith around 500 AD, Teotihuacan was the largest city in the pre-Columbian Americas, with more than two hundred thousand inhabitants, placing it among the largest cities of the world at that time.

Like the two pyramids at Giza, the Pyramid of the Moon at Teotihuacan was built on ground some thirty feet higher than that of the Pyramid of the Sun, giving their peaks the exact same height above sea level. The pyramids at Teotihuacan and Giza also have sides that measure almost the same, 754 feet in Giza and 745 feet at Teotihuacan, and the latter would fit perfectly into the former. The Giza and Teotihuacan pyramids have the exact same base measurement and are all positioned exactly N-S-E-W. These similarities are likely not merely a coincidence. The Teotihuacan pyramids feature steps on the outside, no inner structures, and were built with mud bricks rather than gigantic stones as was the case in Giza.

The Pyramid of the Sun is at the center of all other structures at Teotihuacan, and the other structures encircle (are located) at exactly where the planets in our solar system orbit the sun. This perfect alignment with planetary orbits in our solar system is also evidenced at Stonehenge and Easter Island. This is unbelievable since Nicolaus Copernicus in 1530 AD is generally credited with discovering that the sun, not the earth, is the center of our solar system. Traditional science contends that ancient alignment similarities and accuracy across continents were coincidental but compelling evidence suggests some type of alien assistance. Pictures of Stonehenge and Easter Island megalithic stones are given on the next page.

The Aztecs produced a valuable document called the *Codex Vaticanus* which states there have been five ages or suns on earth. The First Sun, called Matlactli Atl lasted 4,008 years and was characterized by giant people. This First Sun was destroyed by water. We live in the Aztecs' Fifth Sun which they called "The Sun of Movement." The Aztecs used this name because they say the earth will move (pole shift or wobble) and this movement will cause the death of all mankind. The Aztec Fifth Sun began about 4000 BC. The Aztecs did not specify when the "movement" or last day (discussed in chapter 15) would occur, but they believed it would be soon. A map of the Aztec Empire in 1519, two years before Cortes arrived, is provided after the Easter Island picture.

Stonehenge in England

Source: *http://upload.wikimedia.org/wikipedia/commons/2/2e/Stonehenge_-_Wiltonia_sive_Comitatus_Wiltoniensis%3B_Anglice_Wilshire_%28Atlas_van_Loon%29.jpg*

Megalithic Statues on Easter Island in the South Pacific

Source: *http://en.wikipedia.org/wiki/File:Ahu-Akivi-1.JPG*

A Map of the Aztec Empire in the Year 1519

Source: *http://en.wikipedia.org/wiki/*
File:Aztec_Empire_1519_map-fr.svg

A reasonable conclusion from ancient writings is that the Aztecs and Olmecs were truthful rather than imaginary when they reported giants and ancient aliens building large, intricate, astronomically aligned structures. As with the Inca, the Aztecs were likely worshiping Satan and/or fallen angels as gods. There is just no way these ancient people could have done the engineering work or possessed the astrophysics knowledge exhibited at Cholulu, Tenochtitlan, or Teotihuacan without ancient alien assistance. The UFO Aztec connection is quite strong, but let's examine the UFO-Maya link before considering whether the UFO-Christianity connection is fact or fiction.

Chapter 8:
THE UFO-MAYA CONNECTION

The Mayan Empire reigned from about 2000 BC to 900 AD and included the southern Mexican states of Chiapas, Tabasco, and Yucatan as well as Guatemala, Belize, El Salvador, and western Honduras. Today there are more than six million descendants of the Maya but the most authentic of these are the natives that live in a single village, Lacanja Chansayab, Mexico near the Guatemala border. Called the "True People," there are about five hundred Maya natives in this village.

Similar to the Aztec's man/god Quetzalcoatl, Maya writings, stories, carvings, and pictures record that a bearded man/god named Kukulcan appeared to them with twenty of his bearded followers (perhaps fallen angels or Atlanteans). Kukulcan trained the Mayans in everything and promoted goodness and humility and built structures at Chichen Itza (located on the ancient map of Mexico). Kukulcan put an end to human and animal sacrifice, although the Mayas eventually returned to human sacrifice and ritual removal of the heart.

A stone painting of Kukulcan exists on the walls inside a small masonry structure at the north end of Chichen Itza's Great Ball Court. One structure there is called the Temple of the Bearded Man and shows Kukulcan to be a male figure with a Semitic nose and a long, full beard. There are other similar carvings of Kukulcan who left Yucatan toward the west. Sizeable temples that glorify Kukulcan are found at archaeological sites throughout the Yucatan Peninsula and at Chichen Itza, Uxmal, and Mayapan. A picture of a Mayan temple at Chichen Itza is given below. Note how large it is compared to the man walking in front.

A Mayan Temple at Chichen Itza

Source: *http://en.wikipedia.org/wiki/File:Chichen-Itza-Castillo-Seen-From-East.JPG*

The Maya were outstanding astronomers, physicists, and mathematicians and proclaimed to know the exact date of the upcoming "earth movement" to end the Fifth Sun. Their so-called Mesoamerican Long Count Calendar commenced on August 11, 3114 BC, and ends on December 21, 2012. Ironically the year 3100 BC is when the Egyptian civilization suddenly appeared in advanced form. It is highly unlikely that the Olmecs, Maya, or Egyptians ever knew of each other since they lived ten thousand miles and oceans apart. Many scientists use the year 3100 BC as the end of the Stone Age and beginning of the Bronze Age.

The August 11, 3114 BC beginning date also coincides with the founding of Egypt's First Dynasty, the sudden construction of Ireland's oldest prehistoric site at New Grange, the start of work at Stonehenge in England, Troy's earliest archaeological date, the first megalithic construction at Malta, the beginning of Minoan civilization, and the first Indus Valley cities. That date likely is significant in terms of alien (UFO) visitation to the earth. The Hopi Indians of Arizona also believed 12-21-12 would be the end of time, but some evidence suggests that the Hopi may have been a breakaway group of Mayans. A three-minute documentary on the Mayan 12-21-12 last day of their calendar is provided at *http://www.youtube.com/watch?v=D6wI3Pbolb w&feature=related*

Like the Sumerians, the Maya insisted that their predecessors came in UFOs from the Pleiades, a constellation commonly called the Seven Sisters. The Pleiades are mentioned three times in the *Bible* (Job 9:9, 38:31, and Amos 5:8) and are also particularly revered in the Hindu religion. The Maya sacred text, *Popol Vuh,* repeatedly refers to ancient aliens coming to earth from the Pleiades and imparting wisdom to man.

The Maya, like the Aztecs, believed that there had been four ages prior to today's age. Both groups believed the flood ended the fourth age. The Maya believed that the "first men" possessed tremendous knowledge and included giants. The ancient Chinese also recorded that before them were giants – men twice as tall as us who once inhabited the "realm of delight" but lost it by not living "by laws of virtue." A sculpted monolith at the Honduras National Museum obtained from the Maya ceremonial city of Copan depicts the underworld god, Bolon Yokte, who the Maya believed would unleash destructive forces on the world on 12-21-12.

The Maya astonishingly knew and recorded three thousand years ago that on the morning of 12-21-12, the winter solstice sun aligns with the galactic equator, the central line of our galaxy, as it appears from the earth. They miraculously also knew that the earth will "wobble" on its axis on that date. This latter event only occurs every 25,800 years. Maya knowledge of these two upcoming celestial events underscores the credibility of their predictions since modern science first verified these upcoming events in recent decades.

The Mayan Long Count Calendar was actually an astrological almanac that they inherited from the Olmecs who appeared suddenly along the northeast coast of Mexico near Veracruz around 3100 BC and spread down to Izapa near Mexico's border with Guatemala. Even today at Izapa as well as Copan and Chiapas in southernmost Mexico, there remain Olmec ruins and nearby surviving inscriptions of the 2012 prophecy. A picture of the Mayan Long Count Calendar is given below. Note the many interlocking wheels.

The Mayan Long Count Calendar

Source: This picture is in the public domain
viewable at many Web sites, including

(1)

*http://www.google.com/imgres?imgurl=http://jonathanephraim.
files.wordpress.com/2008/07/mayancalendar.jpg&imgrefurl=http://
jonathanephraim.wordpress.com/2008/07/24/12-21-
12/&h=420&w=419&sz=132&tbnid=p-6k2r7loIMcUM:&tbnh
=125&tbnw=125&prev=/images%3Fq%3Dmayan%2Blong%2Bc
ount%2Bcalendar&hl=en&usg=__ttMg38F6H8gNMGEtkezgR_
cpDQQ=&sa=X&ei=yTpKTK7UNYK88gb3w-
E0&ved=0CDQQ9QEwBg and*

(2)

*http://www.google.com/imgres?imgurl=http://i185.photobucket.com/
albums/x271/DukeBuzzy/MayanCalendar.jpg&imgrefurl=http://
picsdigger.com/keyword/mayan%2520long%2520count%2520calendar
/&h=432&w=432&sz=207&tbnid=1eLTEuYh4mIDsM:&tbnh=126&
tbnw=126&prev=/images%3Fq%3Dmayan%2Blong%2Bcount%2Bcal
endar&hl=en&usg=__Rl0GpwNFrEBw9ix2tTiqB8k7Big=&sa=X&ei=
xhQ9TKGyEIG88ga4msDUDg&ved=0CDcQ9QEwBA*

Some scholars contend that the Olmecs were survivors of Atlantis who somehow survived the flood. The Maya legend of the Four Suns describes how death came to their overseas ancestors from out of the sky as it "rained fire upon them" and their ancestors were "swallowed by the waters." Both the *Dresden Codex* and the *Popol Vuh* describe the "drowning of the trees" and how "survivors of the Atlantic cataclysm" built their first post flood temple near the banks of the Huehuhuetan River. The *Popol Vuh* is clear in its assertion that Atlantis was destroyed by the flood and the Maya are descendants of Atlanteans. However, modern science says Atlantis never existed.

At Palenque, the Maya ceremonial center's Temple of Inscriptions contains a stone sarcophagus lid in which the underside is adorned with a carving of their seventh century AD ruler Pacal II at the controls of a UFO. In that carving, Pacal II has a mask on his face, his hands on controls, his left foot is on a pedal, and he is sitting on a chair that has an exhaust trail. The Maya used the carving to depict Pacal descending into the underworld.

Maya knowledge of the 12-21-12 winter solstice alignments, the upcoming wobble on the earth's axis, of giants, and of Atlantis was phenomenal. They must have had some kind of UFO intelligence behind their advanced astrophysics and mathematical knowledge. Perhaps the Maya (or Olmecs or Atlanteans) had contact with some of Satan's fallen angels from the underworld. Satan's forces are extremely knowledgeable and advanced and likely have UFOs for transportation. The Maya may have been worshiping representatives from the underworld. The Maya's *Popol Vuh* accurately describes a clear UFO-Maya connection, but let's examine the ancient Indus Valley civilization as we move on to addressing whether the UFO-Christianity connection is true.

Chapter 9:
THE UFO-INDIA CONNECTION

In 2900 BC, a whole civilization and the Hindu religion itself formed in the northwest area of India in the Indus Valley. The Indus Valley Civilization (IVC) is evidenced by spectacular finds at Mohenjo-Daro, an archaeological site in northwest Sind and at Harappa in central Punjab near the Ravi River. A map of the IVC and the cities just mentioned is given on page 62.

Hinduism has sacred scriptures called the *Vedas,* which people of that religious faith consider to be "not of human origin." There are four books among the *Vedas* which are written in the predecessor of the Indian root-tongue Sanskrit. The similarity between the *Vedas* and the Greek gods and the *Bible* is strikingly close. The *Vedas,* like the Greek writings, say gods are all members of one large family, but not necessarily a peaceful family. The *Vedas* talk about ascents and descents of gods from heaven, aerial UFO battles, wondrous weapons, marriages, infidelities, and excellent recordkeeping of gods' family history. Also analogous to Greek writings, the *Vedas* focus on a pantheon of twelve key gods. Sumerian gods and writings had great influence on Hinduism as well as Greek, Roman, and Egyptian gods, and the *Bible.* People of the Hindu faith even today accept as true all the *Vedas* writings about UFOs and gods.

The Hindu *Vedas* provide many descriptions of UFOs, called Vimanas.

India's national epic, *The Mahabharata*, describes an eighteen-day war between the Kauravas and the Pandavas in which each side used UFOs that delivered weapons of mass destruction. There are repeated references in the *Mahabharata* to great god-kings riding about in Vimanas or "celestial cars," also described as "aerial chariots with sides of iron clad with wings." One recording described Vimanas hurling a single projectile charged with all the power of the universe; an incandescent column of smoke and fire, as brilliant as ten thousand suns, rose in all its splendor that reduced to ashes the entire race of the Vrishnis and Andhakas. Physicist Frederick Soddy studied these writings and said, "I believe there have been civilizations in the past that were familiar with atomic energy, and that by misusing it, they were totally destroyed."

Hitler's Nazi Germany used the *Vedas* to develop advanced flying technologies during World War II. American and British pilots often saw "Foo Fighters" which were UFO balls of light all around their aircraft. Often these balls of light would knock out the electronics on their plane. The Germans also had V1 and V2 cruise missiles developed from the *Vedas*. In the late 1950s, Rudolf Lusar wrote a book titled *German Secret Weapons of World War II* and in that book there is a chapter titled "Wonder Weapons."

A Map of the Indus Valley Showing Key Archealogical Sites

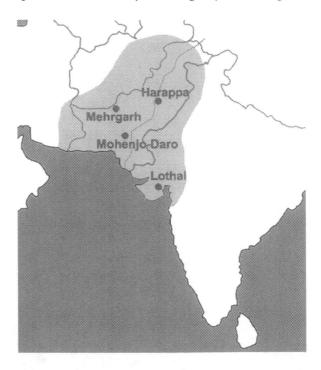

Source: *http://en.wikipedia.org/wiki/File:CiviltàValleIndoMappa.png*

The Hindu sacred books *Samaranga Sutradhara* date back to unknown antiquity and contain 230 stanzas that describe in great detail every possible aspect of UFOs. These writings provide blueprints that detail how UFOs operate, for example, using gyroscopes that spin inside liquid mercury. The ancient Vedic literature describes UFOs as being "fast as thought itself." Sanskrit texts from India are filled with references to gods who fought battles in the sky using Vimanas equipped with deadly weapons. Either the *Vedas* contain some of the earliest known science fiction entertainment, or they record actual conflicts between ancient aliens with weapons as powerful and advanced as anything used today. Coupled with similar information from other civilizations, a reasonable conclusion is that the ancient people of India were reporting, not fabricating, reality.

D.H. Childress and Ivan T. Sanderson in their book *Vimana Aircraft of Ancient India and Atlantis* assert that an ancient civilization in India had made technological advances equaling and perhaps surpassing our own before that civilization was mysteriously destroyed – perhaps in a nuclear war. The Vedic scriptures discuss how the history of humankind is divided into four epochs, or yugas. A great cataclysm ends each yuga. The first epoch was the Krita which lasted 1,728,000 years. The next age was the Treta yuga which lasted 1,296,000 human years. The third yuga was called the Dvapara era which lasted 864,000 human years. Virtually all ancient civilizations knew that "last day" cataclysms had plagued all life on earth in prior millennia.

According to Hindu beliefs, we currently live in the fourth and last yuga called Kali which will last 432,000 years. At the end of this Kali era, the Hindu people believe that a god named Vishnu will return to earth riding a powerful white horse named Kalki, waving a burning sword of destruction. When Vishnu returns, all the people of earth will be judged just as described in the *Bible*. So the Vedic scriptures and the *Bible* are quite similar in many ways. The Vedic scriptures assert that the human race perishes and has to be re-created at the end of each epoch. Also the Vedic scriptures portray mankind as getting more and more immoral, corrupt, wicked, and materialistic with each age. The book of *Revelation* (19:11-19:14) has the same prophecy of an arriving, judging, rider on a white horse.

The Vedic literature says there are four hundred thousand humanlike races of beings living on different planets in the universe and some of these aliens lived on earth in ancient times while some just visited the earth. All aliens traverse the universe in UFOs. The *Vedas* also say our planet was inhabited and controlled by various extraterrestrial races at different times during the last one hundred million years. There are many descriptions and quotes in the Vedic literature referring to aerial machines. For example, it is written that "a man from the great white star took their abode on an Island in the Sea of Gobi in the year of 18,617,841BC." The Vedic documents reveal the following: "On the same day that Krishna departed from earth, the powerful dark-bodied Kali Age descended. The ocean rose and submerged the whole of Dwarka."

Around 26,000 BC, a very advanced civilization called the Rama Empire apparently existed in India and fought wars against another advanced civilization on Atlantis (or Atlas), a country the size of Libya that was lost (destroyed) in the Atlantic Ocean when the flood occurred. Two other continents, Ruta and Lemuria, existed at this time in the Pacific Ocean and Indian Ocean respectively. Like Atlantis, these civilizations supposedly were destroyed when the flood occurred. Giants possibly occupied these continents.

Vedic texts assert that the Rama Empire's most powerful and dangerous enemy were the Atlanteans which had advanced UFOs called Vailixi. The ancient Indians used their Vimanas against the Vailixi. Eklal Kueshana, author of *The Ultimate Frontier*, published an article in 1966 and said, "Vailixi were first developed in Atlantis 20,000 years ago, and the most common ones are saucer shaped at generally trapezoidal cross section with three hemispherical engine ponds on the underside; they use a mechanical antigravity device driven by the engines developing approximately 80,000 horse power."

An archaeological expedition, led by Chi Pu Tei in 1938 in the Baian-Kara-Ula mountains of the Himalayas on the border between China and Tibet discovered a cave with old pictograms of stars and heavens on the wall. They dug there and found a nine-inch disc that consisted of 716 separate plates with hieroglyphics writings. In 1962, Dr. Tsum Um Nui deciphered the disc plate writings which revealed that a UFO manned by aliens who called themselves Dropa crashed nearby around 10,000 BC and took refuge in the caves. The plates said the Dropa were unable to repair their disabled spacecraft and could not return to their home planet near the star Sirius, so they began living and breeding with humans on earth. Early Chinese texts provide details on how to build a flying craft, including texts from the Emperor Shun era between 2258 BC and 2208 BC and also from the even Emperor Cheng Tang era around 1766 BC.

Relatively close to earth in terms of stars, Sirius A is twice as bright as the next brightest star in the sky and is twice the size of our sun. There is a tribe of people called the Dogon that live today near Timbuktu in Africa. For more than seven hundred years, the elders of this tribe have proclaimed that a UFO landed many years ago near them and the aliens gave the Dogon extensive information about their home star Sirius B. For example, the Dogon were told that the rotation of Sirius B around Sirius A takes 50.1 years. The Dogon even knew that Sirius B is a white dwarf star and that one cubic inch of that star was to weigh two thousand pounds. Sirius A is situated to the left and straight down from the belt of Orion. A direct line from the three bright stars in Orion's belt takes you right to Sirius A. Scientists did not discover the existence of Sirius B until 1970, but the Dogon astonishingly knew details about Sirius B seven hundred years ago.

The Indian Vedic literature contains more extensive information about UFOs than any other ancient civilization, followed closely by the Sumerian writings. Recall that prior to Sumerian times (3800 BC) nothing was written down, just stories and pictures and carvings were passed down to descendants. The ancient people in India surely did not make up all the detailed UFO information, so the UFO-India connection is very compelling and actually represents the absolute truth for all of the Hindu faith today. Before moving onto UFO-Christianity issues, however, let's examine the UFO-Atlantis connection - which the ancient Indus Valley people and their *Vedas* (and other ancient writings) refer to so often.

Chapter 10:
THE UFO-ATLANTIS CONNECTION

Although modern science does not (yet) acknowledge Atlantis, many ancient writings clearly say Atlantis was the capital city of Atlas, a large island in the Atlantic Ocean. According to *The Atlantis Encyclopedia*, by 13,000 BC the Atlantean Empire stretched from the Americas to the western shores of North Africa, the British Isles, Iberia, and Italy and as far as the Aegean coasts of Asia Minor. The Atlanteans reportedly dominated the Bronze Age but their empire eventually clashed with powerful Greek interests in the Aegean, resulting in a long war. Eventually the Greeks pushed the Atlantean invaders out of the Mediterranean world. Then the flood occurred that simultaneously destroyed Atlantis and the pursuing Greek armies who had gathered in present-day Morocco. Most ancient writings and substantial evidence support this narrative about Atlantis.

Famous writer and philosopher, Edgar Cayce, often called the twentieth-century's Sleeping Prophet, repeatedly emphasized in his written and spoken word that the people of Atlantis (Atlanteans) were the inventors of a technology superior to twentieth-century accomplishments. He describes the Atlanteans as having submarines, spacecraft, and having mastered nuclear fission and all aspects of electrical and chemical energies. Edgar Cayce said the Atlanteans possessed "things of transportation, the aeroplane, as called today, and ships of the air, for they sailed not only in the air but in other elements also" (Cayce 2437-

1, 1/23/41). Cayce's view of Atlantis matched quite well descriptions of Atlantis in the *Vedas*.

A picture of Edgar Cayce as he looked in 1910 is given below. Born in 1877, Cayce was an American psychic who, while in a self-induced trance, could provide answers to questions on subjects such as Atlantis. Cayce was a founder of the New Age Movement and a lifelong member of the Christian denomination Disciples of Christ. Today, members of Cayce's organization, the Association for Research and Enlightenment (ARE), exist worldwide, and Edgar Cayce Centers are found in more than thirty-five countries.

A Picture of Edgar Cayce in 1910

Source: *http://en.wikipedia.org/wiki/File:Cayce_1910.jpg*

Born in 428 BC in Athens or Aegina, the Greek philosopher Plato described Atlantis as a highly civilized culture in the Atlantic Ocean that flourished before the rise of other civilizations and succumbed to a natural catastrophe. Plato's writings are the best documents available on Atlantis, which he said was located outside the Straits of Gibraltar. Plato lists the ten former kings of Atlantis. A famous painting of Plato done by Italian painter Raffaello Sanzio in 1509 is given on the next page. Plato was a mathematician, writer, and founder of the Academy in Athens, considered by scholars to be the first institution of higher learning or college in the world. Plato's mentor was Socrates and his student was Aristotle.

The *Vedas* from ancient India speak repeatedly about Atlantis as does the *Popol Vuh* which describes the Hun yecil, – the Drowning of the Trees – and the U Mamae, or Old Men, survivors of the Atlantis cataclysm who built their first post-flood temple near the banks of the Huehuhuetan River, in thanks to the gods for their escape. Atlantean survivors of the flood perhaps arrived as culture bearers to the Olmecs, Inca, Maya, Aztecs, Egyptians, and Sumerians. Perhaps survivors of the Atlantean population carried stories of the flood to peoples around the globe, who then passed these stories on to future generations.

A Famous Painting of Plato

Source: *http://en.wikipedia.org/wiki/File:Plato-raphael.jpg*

Colonel James Churchward studied the lost island of Lemuria, sometimes called Mu. He discovered in Lhasa, Tibet, perhaps the oldest tablets made by man that supposedly contained the original language of humankind. Churchward was convinced that the tablets he discovered were authentic. He named them the Lhasa Tablets. At an altitude of 11,450 feet, Lhasa is one of the highest capitals in the world, is the birthplace of Tibetan Buddhism, and means "place of the gods." Provided on the next page is a map showing Lemuria and Atlantis. You can see how refugees from these two continents may have spread out after the flood to carry stories globally. Lemurians and Atlanteans who survived the flood potentially also "educated" the known world.

A Map Showing Lemuria and Atlantis

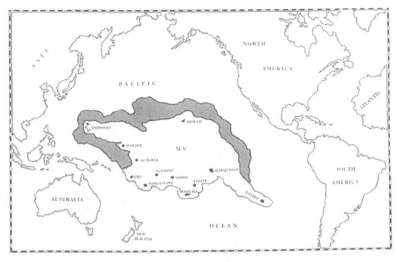

THE GEOGRAPHICAL POSITION OF MU

Source: *http://en.wikipedia.org/wiki/File:Book_map1.jpg*

From the tablets, Churchward determined that Lemuria had seven wonderful cities and many overseas colonies. Lemurians looked like humans except were much taller than modern man and superior to us in science and technology. There were reportedly sixty-four million Lemurians. The Lhasa tablets say Lemuria was destroyed by a cataclysmic event and all people perished. The Lhasa tablets describe the last moments as follows:

"When the star Bal fell into the earth at a place where there is nothing but sea, the seven cities with their temples and their golden gates were shaken, a great fire sprang up, and the streets were filled with dense smoke. Men trembled with fear, and great crowds flocked to the temples and the king's palace. The king said to them, "Did I not predict all this?" and the men and women in the precious garments and bracelets begged and implored him: Ra-Mu, save us. But the king told them that they were all doomed to die with their slaves and children, and that a new race of mankind would rise from their ashes." (p. 168 in Ellen Lloyd's *Voices from Legendary Times*).

The Lhasa tablets reveal that the people were unaware of the coming disaster, but the king knew of it. It is interesting that in flood stories from around the world, the gods always knew about the approaching cataclysm, but the people never knew until doom happened. It is possible that the king of Mu was of extraterrestrial origin, perhaps a fallen angel.

The pre-Columbian Mayan text called the *Troana Codex* described the destruction of Mu as follows: "There occurred terrible earthquakes, which continued without interruption until the thirteenth Chuen. The country of the hills of mud, and the land of Mu, was sacrificed. Being twice upheaved, it suddenly disappeared during the night, the basin being continually shaken by the volcanic forces. Being confined, these earthquakes caused the land to sink, and to rise several times in various places. At last the surface gave way and ten countries were torn asunder and scattered. Unable to stand the force of the convulsion, they sank with their sixty-four million inhabitants 8,060 years before the writing of this book."

Underwater archeologists have discovered roads, monuments, and cities that for many scholars say confirm the existence and later the destruction of Atlantis and Lemuria. The huge limestone blocks that comprise the underwater Bimini Roads off the North Bimini Island in the Bahamas are one example. After extensive study, Veda Carlson in 1970 wrote *The Great Migration* and said, "Lemuria was a continent in the Pacific. A fourth and final cataclysmic event was the catastrophe of twelve thousand years ago that sent Lemuria and millions of her people to the depths in a "vortex of fire and water." Plato wrote that Atlantis was destroyed in 11,500 BC. Cayce often described the Lemurians as peaceful and introverted, whereas the Atlanteans he said were aggressive and outgoing. Cayce said the Lemurians were more religious and spiritual oriented whereas the Atlanteans were more technologically oriented. A ten-minute documentary on Atlantis is provided at the Web site *http://www.youtube.com/watch?v=kTEOM_ZzKKk&feature=related*

Substantial evidence suggests that the lost civilizations of Atlantis and Lemuria were headquarters of ancient alien visitors to earth thousands of years before the flood killed virtually all of them. Perhaps these civilizations arose after the Toba volcanic eruption on Sumatra in 73,000 BC. Plato, Cayce, and other scholars, as well as the *Vedas*, record clearly that these two civilizations had UFO vehicles and thus possessed high-tech astronomical and mathematical knowledge of the type exhibited at various pyramids and megalithic sites around the globe. Perhaps survivors of the Atlantean and/or Lemurian civilizations imparted their knowledge to these other cultures. That would explain twenty-first-century-type sophistication exhibited at places such as Giza and Puma Punku, as well as the Maya Long Count Calendar. But before drawing conclusions, let's examine a few other issues, such as the flood, to determine its relationship to the eventual UFO-Christianity connection that this book seeks to clarify.

Chapter 11:
THE UFO-FLOOD CONNECTION

Virtually every civilization on every continent independently passed down stories or wrote about the Deluge or Great Flood. The actual date of the flood can be debated. For example, biblical Noah was supposedly born in 3998 BC and died in 3048 BC but there is no geological evidence to support a global catastrophe during that time. D.S. Allan and J.B. Delair wrote a book titled *Cataclysm: Compelling Evidence of a Cosmic Catastrophe in 9,500 BC* in which they compile more than five hundred flood stories from Europe, Asia, Africa, Australia, and the Americas.

Geologists and archaeologists know a worldwide comet storm calamity occurred about 10,900 BC and started a 1,300 year-long-ice age. University of Oregon professor Douglas Kennett in the journal *Science* (January 2009) provides evidence for this catastrophe. Just one large meteorite hitting in the ocean could cause mile-high tsunamis worldwide. Also called the Younger Dryas or the Big Freeze, this comet impact of 10,900 BC resulted in all of Scandinavia's forests becoming tundra, and most of the Middle East becoming desert. In North America, the Clovis culture, an early society of Paleo-Indians, was nearly wiped out on that day and never recovered.

Geologic records reveal that every ice age that has occurred in earth's long history began abruptly with some cataclysmic event that wiped out many life-forms. There is substantial evidence also that this comet storm around 10,900 BC may have caused a pole shift whereby the North Pole shifted from the Hudson Bay area to its present location in the Artic Ocean. Called a "geomagnectic reversal," pole shifts complete themselves in about twenty hours as the earth's land masses change dramatically with winds approaching one thousand miles per hour for twenty hours, destroying most life in a global flooding event.

It is widely known that before 10,900 BC, humans fished fresh water lakes in the state of Utah. However as the flood receded, ocean water created the Great Salt Lake in Utah. The salt in that lake is not just plain salt, it is ocean salt, with all the minerals of ocean salt. Native American stories talk about survivors of the flood in high elevations seeing a gigantic tsunami covering all lower levels of land. For thirty-five minutes at *http://www.youtube.com/watch?v=-nNZOjDi_dQ&feature=related*, Rhawn Joseph, Ph.D discusses scientific evidence for the flood about 10,900 BC and its impact on life.

After the flood, it took roughly seven thousand years for the Tigris-Euphrates plain (Iraq) to sufficiently dry out from the mud and sludge for the Sumerian civilization to begin. Flood stories were already prevalent among the Incas and Aztecs way before the Spaniards arrived. All the flood stories from across the planet speak of a god displeased with human behavior, instructing a certain individual to build a craft or ark, and then destroying mankind with the flood, and then creating a new and improved human. In Egypt, it was the Sun god Ra who caused the flood upon the people of earth. In China, the man who was saved from the flood was Nu-wah, a name not that different from Noah. The Greek flood story tells how Zeus, their highest god, destroyed humans with the flood.

Virtually all ancient stories say God brought about the flood also to kill the offspring of fallen angels, as well as the giants. Only small groups of humans survived the flood, including Noah and his family (wife, three sons, and their wives) in the ark. Very few animals, plants, and people survived. People after the flood reportedly lived less than one hundred years compared to about nine hundred years before the flood, as recorded in Genesis 11.

The Aztec's *Mexica-Nahuatl* timetable dates the flood to about 10,900 BC. A sampling of evidence from this catastrophe is that mammoths and many other animals such as the saber-toothed tiger instantly became extinct on a single day worldwide about that time. Scientists have determined that thousands of mammoths were eating plants when the catastrophe occurred. Before the plants could even be digested, the animals were frozen solid. Scientists can also tell that on this day the mammoths were being torn and twisted apart by a very violent force such as a flood or earthquake. Dr. Frank Hibbon, professor of the archaeology of the University of New Mexico, researched Alaskan mammoths and writes:

"Within the mass, frozen solid, lie the twisted parts of animals and trees intermingled with lenses of ice and layers of pear and mosses. It looks as though in the middle of some catastrophe of ten thousand years ago the whole Alaskan world of living animals and plants was suddenly frozen in mid-motion...dumped in all attitudes of death ... Legs and torsos and heads and fragments were found together in piles or scattered separately . . animals were torn apart and scattered over the landscape even though they may have weighed several tons ..." (p. 200 from Ellen Lloyd's *Voices of Legendary Times*).

A picture of a mammoth is given on the next page. Note how large this animal was compared to the child underneath. Large male mammoths could reach a height of sixteen feet tall and weigh twelve tons. They lived from 4.8 million years ago to 4,500 years also when the last few died off. Not just mammoths, but the remains of whole schools of ocean fish and seashells have been uncovered on the tops of the world's highest mountains and dated to have died virtually at the same time. Archaeologists have discovered human skeletons also mixed together with animal bones on hills and mountains all over the world. People and animals apparently did their best to flee the flood, but with little to no warning nearly all were unable to survive. Prior to the 10,900 BC event, Siberia and Alaska had a rather warm environment but this event instantly began a severe mini-ice age worldwide. According to the Aztecs, the cosmic catastrophe responsible for the flood dropped the earth into cold, darkness for twenty-five years.

A Mammoth Life-Size Reconstruction

Source: *http://upload.wikimedia.org/wikipedia/*
commons/9/9c/Mammoth_Mammut_model.JPG

The Eskimos of Greenland passed down stories of when the earth "turned over." They say the constellation of the Cold Bears tried to plunge into the water. The American Pawnee Indians remember when the North Polar star and the South Polar star "changed places" or as they say "went to see each other." A geomagnetic reversal such as described could have occurred with passage nearby or impact of a large asteroid, according to Austrian meteorologists Julius Hann and many others. Whatever the cause, the flood was reported in ancient writings to be greatly feared by ancient aliens (or gods) on earth who knew the flood was coming and left in UFOs the day before - without telling mankind. Most animal and plant life on earth was decimated, including giants. Let's talk about giants a moment before addressing the UFO-Christianity connection.

Chapter 12:
THE UFO-GIANTS CONNECTION

Skeletons of giants have been found practically everywhere, including North and South America, Europe, Asia, Australia, and Africa. Homo sapiens appeared on the planet about 400,000 BC, perhaps including giants up to eighteen feet tall. Bones from giant humanoids have been found all over the planet, including some in the Grand Canyon of Arizona by Samuel Hubbard in 1896. On August 5, 1947, archaeologist Howard E. Hill discovered thirty-two caves in a 180-square–mile area in California's Death Valley and southern Nevada. The caves contained mummies of nine-foot-tall men who lived 80,000 years ago. Abbe Pegues wrote in his work *The Volcanoes of Greece* that "near the volcanoes of the Isles of Thera, giants with enormous skulls have been found." There are bones from giant humans on display at the Mt. Blanco Fossil Museum in Crosbyton, Texas, as illustrated on the next page.

The Old Testament describes the Nephilim as a race of giants who ruled the world before the flood. Deuteronomy 2:11 says the descendants of the Nephilim were the Emim, Rephaim, or Anakim, "a people great, and many, and tall." Quite a few *Bible* verses refer to giants, such as Deuteronomy 2:10, 2:11, 2:20, 2:21, 3:11, 3:13, and Joshua 12:4, 13:12, 15:8, 17:15, and 18:16. The story of David and Goliath is in 1 Samuel 17. Genesis 6:4 says: "There were giants in the earth in those days; and also after that, when the sons of God came in unto the daughters of men, and they bare children to them, the same became mighty men which were of old, men of renown." The Catholic patron saint of travel, St. Christopher, stood nearly eighteen feet tall. Eastern Catholic churches acknowledge this but western churches do not. As the story goes, Christopher devoted his life to carrying people across an otherwise impassable stream. One day a little child appeared before him and asked to be carried across. To Christopher's surprise, as he forded the river, the child steadily increased in weight until he became too heavy to carry. When Christopher asked the holy child why he weighed so much, the child replied that he carried the world's sins upon his shoulders. As a reward for his service, Christopher's staff was miraculously transformed into a living tree.

Book of Enoch 9:7-10 says, "And the women became pregnant and gave birth to great giants whose heights were three hundred cubits. These giants consumed the produce of all the people until the people detested feeding them. So the giants turned against the people in order to eat them. And they began to sin against birds, wild beasts, reptiles, and fish…" Numbers 13:33 says, "And there we saw the giants, the sons of Anak, which come of the giants: and we were in our own sight as grasshoppers, and so we were in their sight."

Forty miles west of Niagara Falls in the town of Cayuga, the remains of nearly two hundred nine-foot-tall individuals were discovered as reported by *The Daily Telegraph* of Toronto in 1873. A similar find was recorded in Lovelock Cave which is seventy miles northeast of Reno, Nevada. Skeletal remains of giants have been discovered and recorded in many counties in Ohio, including Noble, Erie, Lawrence, and Monroe.

A 47-inch human femur bone is pictured on the next page.

The Forty-Seven Inch Human Femur Bone

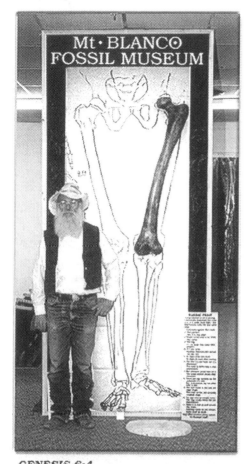

47 inch Human Femur

In the late 1950s, during road construction in south-east Turkey in the Euphrates Valley, many tombs containing the remains of Giants were uncovered. At two sites the leg bones were measured to be about 120 cms "47.24 inches". Joe Taylor, Director of the Mt. BLANCO FOSSIL MUSEUM in Crosbyton, Texas, was commissioned to sculpt this anatomically correct, and to scale, human femur. This "Giant" stood some 14-16 feet tall, and had 20-22 inch long feet. His or Her finger tips, with arms to their sides, would be about 6 feet above the ground. The Biblical record, in Deuteronomy 3:11 states that the Iron Bed of Og, King of Bashan was 9 cubits by 4 cubits or approximately 14 feet long by 6 feet wide!

GENESIS 6:4 ——————————————————————
There were Nephilim (Giants) in the earth in those days; and also after that when the sons of God (Angels?) came in unto the daughters of men, and they bare children to them, the same became mighty men which were of old, men of renown.

More Info & Replicas available at mtblanco1@aol.com or www.mtblanco.com
Mt. Blanco Fossil Museum • P.O. Box 559, Crosbyton, TX 79322 • 1-800-367-7454

Source: *www.mtblanco.com* Written permission obtained from Joe Taylor, director of the Mt. Blanco Fossil Museum.

Many of the American Indian nations including the Piute, Pawnee, Shoshone, Cherokee, and Iroquois, passed down numerous stories about giant people ravaging their settlements. The Pawnee believed the earth was first inhabited by a race of giants so large that they could carry buffaloes on their backs. According to the history of the Iroquois Nation, prehistoric giants were enemies to Native American Indians.

A possible scenario regarding giants is that fallen angels supervised by Satan created giant humans up to twenty feet tall by impregnating Neanderthal women. People became slaves to and ultimately food for these humanoid giants. Giants were involved in ancient alien's mining operations and in building megalithic structures all over the planet. It is possible if not probable that the Yeti, Bigfoot, abominable snowman, and Sasquatch are giants who on occasion today exit the earth's underworld and make themselves visible to people. These ape-like creatures appear most often in the Pacific Northwest of the USA and in the Himalayas and are variously described as standing seven to ten feet tall and weighing over five hundred pounds, with footprints seventeen inches long. A map of North America is given on the next page that shows the number of Bigfoot sightings per region. Note that the state of Washington has the most sightings followed by California.

Color Coded North America Map of Bigfoot Sightings
(Darker Colors Indicate Greater Number of Sightings)

Source: *http://en.wikipedia.org/wiki/Bigfoot*

Gigantopithecus and meganthropus are names given to giant hominids found by paleontologists and carbon dated to 1 million BC. Meganthropus occupied Southeast Asia over a million years ago. In their book *Forbidden Archaeology*, Michael Cretno and Richard Thompson assert that people similar to us lived as far back as 55 million years ago. On August 14, 1880, an article appeared in the *Scientific American* reporting the discovery of a graveyard of giant people. The article reads:

"The Rev. Stephen Bowers notes in the *Kansas City Review of Science* the opening of an interesting mound in Brush Creek Township, Ohio. The mound was opened by the Historical Society of the township, under the immediate supervision of Dr. J.F. Everhart, of Zanesville. It measured sixty-four by thirty-five feet at the summit, gradually sloping in every direction, and was eight feet in height. There was found in it a sort of clay coffin including the skeleton of a woman measuring eight feet in length. In another grave was found the skeleton of a man and a woman, the former measuring nine and the latter eight feet in length. In a third grave were two skeletons, male and female, measuring respectively nine feet four inches and eight feet. Seven other skeletons were found in the mound, the smallest of which measured eight feet, while others reached the enormous length of ten feet."

Just as ancient cultures passed down stories and writings about UFOs and the flood, they did the very same for giants. Noah who lived from 3998 BC to 3048 BC was supposedly the last of the pre-flood giants. He and his wife, three sons, and their wives built the ark and survived the flood along with the animals in the ark. Both biblical and archeological evidence suggests that giants surely once inhabited the earth. Some giants may still exist in the underworld and at times exit through mountain crevices and then seemingly vanish back into the crevices. Nearly all reports say these creatures smell like sulfur, which would be consistent with living in the underworld. If they are fallen angels, they may be godlike rather than apelike which would explain why traditional means of tracking and hunting these creatures have been ineffective.

Three- and ten-minute videos respectively that provide archeological evidence for giants may be watched at various Web sites, including: *http://www.youtube.com/watch?v=B8bVEIVUh8&feature=related http:// www.youtube.com/watch?v=18CY7ZaCfzY&feature=related*

The connection between UFOs and giants is quite possible because ancient writings indicate that fallen angels and/or ancient aliens in UFOs interbred with prehistoric man purposefully to produce giants – perhaps to do the hard work of mining. Sometimes fallen angels are referred to as sons of God. Before drawing conclusions regarding UFOs and Christianity, let's examine the notion of "sons of God" a bit further.

Chapter 13:
THE UFO-SONS OF GOD CONNECTION

The term "son of God" was never used in the Old Testament but was used forty-three times in the New Testament, always referencing Jesus. Of the forty-three times however, Jesus referred to himself only four times as the son of God and all four are in the Gospel according to John. More commonly used was the term "son of man" that was used eighty-six times in the New Testament and one hundred sixteen times in the Old Testament. Jesus almost always referred to himself as the "son of man." Under heavy criticism from a mob of religious leaders however, Jesus on one occasion is quoted in John 10:31 saying, "I am the Son of God."

The term "sons of God" appears six times in the Old Testament and five in the New Testament. For example, Genesis 6:1-4 refers to "sons of God" as mighty, renowned men of an ancient origin who were famous and infatuated with women. These sons of God produced offspring so apparently they were indeed physical beings. Job 1:6 says, "Now there was a day when the sons of God came to present themselves before the Lord, and Satan also came among them…" Job 38:7 says, "When the morning stars sang together, and all the sons of God shouted for joy." Jesus apparently was intent on making sure the people of his time did not confuse him with the fallen angels as the "sons of God."

Sumerian writings as well as the *Bible* say the sons of God began taking daughters of men as wives. Due to a warm climate, the gods likely used Nippur and Sippar in Sumeria (Iraq) as headquarters and used Bad-Tibira nearby as a metallurgical center for smelting and refining. They simultaneously likely used the Tiahuanacu and Nazca areas in Peru as mining centers to obtain gold and tin, as well as South Africa. The ancient Zulus in South Africa, and some scientists today, date many South African mines as being over one hundred thousand years old. An excellent Web site with plenty of pictures, narrative, and documentation about mining operations two hundred thousand years ago in South Africa is: *http://viewzone2.com/adamscalendarx.html.*

Ancient writings assert consistently and strongly that ancient aliens wanted to avoid the hard work associated with mining and thus used artificial insemination to create humans and giants and used both as primitive workers in the mines. Quite likely therefore man was originally developed to be primitive workers, rather than being created to worship gods. Evolution of the human species likely occurred just as anthropologists say, except for one big exception - there was an ancient alien intervention thousands of years ago that leapfrogged human evolution from the stone-age to modern people.

In the *Book of Enoch,* eighteen angels are named as chief participators in the conspiracy to mate with women. Samiaza and Azael are leaders. Azael imparts to men all sorts of useful as well as secret knowledge and the art of beautifying eyes. Luke 10:18 and Revelation 12:7-10 reveal that "Satan and certain angels rebelled against God, or through weakness under temptation, forfeited their angelic dignity and were degraded and condemned to a life of mischief or shame on earth or in a place of punishment. Satan fell from heaven "with the velocity of lightning." Originally Satan was one of God's angels who lusted for worldly power and was exiled. Samael (Genesis 25) was originally the chief of God's angels but became the angel of death and the "chieftain of all the Satans" (Deuteronomy 9, Matthew 25:41). Naamah, the wife of Noah (Genesis 23:3), was one of the women whose great beauty tempted the angels to sin (Genesis 4:22). As regards to Azazel and Samazai, it was a young woman named Istar or Esther that proved fatal to their virtue. These angels, seeing God's grief over the corruption of the sons of men (Genesis 6:2-7), volunteered to descend to earth.

According to the *Book of Enoch*, the original watchers numbered a total of two hundred and their leaders are named. The book says the "watchers" were angels dispatched to earth simply to watch over mankind. They soon begin to lust for human women and eventually defect in mass to illicitly instruct and procreate among humanity. The children produced by these unions are the Nephilim, savage giants who pillage the earth and endanger humanity. The *Book of Enoch* says Samyaza and associates taught humans about arts, weaponry, cosmetics, mirrors, and sorcery, which were intended to be discovered gradually over time, not foisted upon humanity all at once. Eventually God allows the flood to rid the earth of the Nephilim, but first sends Uriel to warn Noah of the pending flood, so as not to totally eradicate the human race. Jude says the watchers themselves are bound "in the valleys of the earth" until Judgment Day (Genesis 6:4 and Jude 1:6). The "watchers" story in Enoch is similar to the sixth chapter of Genesis where it describes the "Origin of the Nephilim" and mentions the "Sons of God" who beget them:

> Genesis 6:1-4: When men began to multiply on earth and daughters were born to them, the sons of God saw how beautiful the daughters of man were, and so they took for their wives as many of them as they chose. Then the Lord said, "My spirit shall not remain in man forever, since he is but flesh. His days shall comprise one hundred and twenty years."

The *Book of Enoch* regards the fallen angels as the Benei Ha-Elohim (Sons of God) in Genesis. Leaders among the watchers mentioned in 1 Enoch include Semiazaz, their leader, Arakiba, Râmêêl, Kokabiel, Tamiel, Ramiel, Danel, Ezeqeel, Baraqijal, Asael, Armaros, Batarel, Ananel, Zaqiel, Samsapeel, Satarel, Turel, Jomjael, Sariel These are the leaders of two hundred fallen angels in 1 Enoch who mated with human women and revealed forbidden knowledge.

The *Book of Enoch* says Araqiel taught humans the signs of the earth. Azazel taught men to make knives, swords, shields, and how to devise ornaments and cosmetics. Gadriel taught the art of cosmetics. Baraqel taught men astrology. Bezaliel taught men meterology. Kokabiel is a high-ranking, holy angel but, in general apocryphal lore and also in Enoch I, he is a fallen watcher and commands 365,000 surrogate spirits to do his bidding. Among other duties, he instructs his fellows in astrology. Penemue "taught mankind the art of writing with ink and paper" and taught "the children of men the bitter and the sweet and the secrets of wisdom." Sariel taught mankind about the courses of the moon (at one time regarded as forbidden knowledge). Samyaza is one of the leaders of the fall from heaven. Shamsiel, once a guardian of Eden and one of the two chief aides to the archangel Uriel (the other aide being Hasdiel), is a fallen angel who teaches man the signs of the sun.

Since God used watchers once, he may still use watchers today to oversee mankind, although these previous watchers are now confined to the underworld. Perhaps God's new watchers today are guardian angels that traverse the earth's skies in UFOs as needed. These watchers today may take care of mankind - performing miracles, answering prayers, monitoring Satan and the underworld, and/or whatever duties God has assigned to them. God's watchers today perhaps use earth's moon as their home base. Evidence from the Apollo moon voyages indicates that UFOs regularly come and go from the moon.

The Apollo 11 space flight to the moon launched from Cape Canaveral on July 20, 1969 and landed the first humans on the moon on July 20, 1969. The Apollo 11 crew included Commander Neil Armstrong, Command Module Pilot Michael Collins, and Lunar Module Pilot Buzz Aldrin Jr. On July 20, Armstrong and Aldrin landed in the Sea of Tranquility and became the first humans to walk on the moon. Their landing craft, *Eagle*, spent twenty-one hours and thirty-one minutes on the lunar surface, while Collins orbited above in the command ship, *Columbia*. The three astronauts returned to Earth with 47.5 pounds of lunar rocks and landed in the Pacific Ocean on July 24. Five subsequent Apollo missions also landed astronauts on the moon, the last in December 1972. In six Apollo spaceflights, twelve men walked on the moon.

Several YouTube documentaries about the Apollo 11 mission are given below, revealing that the moon may be home base for UFOs. Other similar videos, not included here, are available for the other Apollo moon missions.

Former NASA Employees Describe UFO Moon Bases
http://www.youtube.com/watch?v=x2qaZFC2PtM&NR=1

Buzz Aldrin explains how a UFO traveled beside Apollo 11 on its way to the moon.
http://www.youtube.com/watch?v=XlkV1ybBnHI&NR=1

Buzz Aldrin reveals there is a "god made" structure on a moon of Mars. He says, "the universe put it there, or if you choose, god put it there," referring to an alien built structure.
http://www.youtube.com/watch?v=bDIXvpjnRws&feature=related

Neil Armstrong tells kids on the 25th anniversary of that first moon landing: "there are great breakthroughs for those who can remove truths protective layers" – perhaps referring to a NASA cover-up.
http://www.youtube.com/watch?v=DplDreUFcEM&feature=related

A National Geographic documentary on the Apollo 11 moon landing
http://www.youtube.com/watch?v=iSPQTfp5vJE&feature=related

In summary, ancient writings indicate that sons of God were originally dispatched, presumably in UFOs, to be watchers over mankind, but they became fallen angels for violating God's commands. That is likely why Jesus generally referred to himself as the son of man so as not to be confused with the sons of God or fallen angels. The *Book of Enoch* provides much greater detail for the biblical notion of fallen angels and watchers. God may use watchers today, perhaps guardian angels, who use the moon as home base for their UFOs. UFOs seen on the Apollo missions likely therefore would **Not** be associated with the underworld or Satan.

Chapter 14:
THE UFO-UNDERWORLD CONNECTION

Researcher John Chitty may have it correct when he writes: "In probing the mountain of data on UFOs, one finds that almost 50 percent of all UFO sightings have taken place over water, coming out of water, plunging into water, navigating underwater, coming from the direction of large bodies of water, or traveling towards large bodies of water. It is possible therefore that these aquatic sightings actually depict the underworld (fallen angels, Satan, giants) covert activity on the surface of this planet as they come and go from deep crevices in the earth's crust. This would leave God's new watchers as the remaining 50 percent of UFO sightings taking place on the surface of this world" (p. 285 from *The Broken Bible*). In other words, half the UFOs seen today may be "good" and half may be "bad." God's watchers in their UFOs today could be involved even in activities such as managing souls as individuals die and/or keeping God informed as he takes care of business traversing the universe.

Either God was the winner of celestial wars and Satan was the loser, or Satan and his fallen angels rebelled against God and were exiled. Either way, ancient writings suggest that Satan and the fallen angels are today largely confined to the underworld. Revelation 12:4, 7, and 9 says, "And there was war in heaven: Michael and his angels fought against the dragon; and the dragon fought along with his angels, And prevailed not; neither was their place found any more in heaven. And the great dragon was cast out, that old serpent, called the Devil, and Satan, which deceiveth the whole world: he was cast out into the earth, and his angels were cast out with him."

The ancient Mayans, Egyptians, and Sumerians idolized the snake, serpent, and dragon - all biblical symbols of Satan. These people wore headdresses and crowns of these animals. The Mayans incorporated the snake or serpent into the actual design of their pyramids. The Mayans and Egyptians both idolized two spotted cats, the jaguar and leopard respectively. These animals are the symbolic embodiment of Osiris - god of the underworld. The spotted cat is also a trademark of the constellation Orion. The Leopard/Osiris is one of the four animals found in the beast mentioned in Revelation. These animals supposedly will come rising up (in UFOs) out of the sea (underworld) to devour mankind during the days of the Great Judgment.

The Egyptians believed the lion to be sacred. The lower half of the Great Sphinx is the body of a lion. Likely the upper half of that structure was originally also a lion. The lion is one of the four animals that make up the terrifying beasts of Revelation. In essence, the lion was one of the four leaders of a third of the constellations that rebelled against God in the universe. Leo the Lion (Ra), Orion the Leopard (Osiris), Draco the Dragon (Satan). The *Bible* refers often to the underworld, such as in Job 1:6-7: "Now there was a day when the sons of God came to present themselves before the LORD, and Satan came also among them. And the LORD said unto Satan, Whenst comest thou? Then Satan answered the LORD, and said, From going to and fro in the earth, and from walking up and down in it."

Daniel 7:2-7 Daniel spake and said, I saw in my vision by night, and, behold, the four winds of the heaven strove upon the great sea. And four great beasts came up from the sea, diverse one from another. The first was like a lion, and had eagle's wings: I beheld till the wings upon the feet as a man, and a man's heart was given to it. And behold another beast, a second, like to a bear, and it raised up itself on one side, and it had three ribs in the mouth of it between the teeth of it and they said thus unto it, Arise, devour much flesh. After this I beheld, and lo another, like a leopard, which had upon the back of it four wings of a fowl; the beast had also four heads, and dominion was given to it. After this I saw in the night visions, and behold a fourth beast dreadful and terrible, and strong exceedingly; and it had great iron teeth: it devoured and brake in pieces, and stamped the residue with the feet of it: and it was diverse from all the beasts that were before it; and it had ten horns.

Daniel 7:17-18 These great beasts, which are four, are four kings, which shall arise out of the earth. But the saints of the most High shall take the kingdom, and possess the kingdom forever, even forever and ever.

Revelation 13:2 And the beast which I saw was like unto a leopard, and his feet were as the feet of a bear, and his mouth as the mouth of a lion: and the dragon gave him his power, and his seat, and great authority.

The four beasts above match up to the four star systems (constellations) that apparently rebelled against God: Draco (the Dragon), Ursa Major/ Minor (the Bear), Leo (Lion/Ra), and Orion (the Leopard). Stories, pictures, sculptures, and writings from ancient civilizations indicate that Satan's domain in the universe before he and the fallen angels were exiled was the particular constellations named above. God has dominion over the whole universe now and perhaps spends most of his time patrolling and managing distant galaxies, stars, and planets – one of which may be his home - heaven, wherever that is located, perhaps Sirius A or the Pleiades. It is possible that God may love the earth so much that he keeps in check various alien civilizations in the universe that could threaten earth. It is more than just conceivable that God likely has watchers, angels on earth today, who may actually use the moon as their UFO spaceport as they monitor humanity. Recall that the astronauts who went to the moon reported significant Santa Claus activity.

A reasonable conclusion is that God will one day release the fallen angels and Satan with their UFOs from the underworld within the earth. Or God may know that the underworld forces will be released on a certain day due to earth's galactic sun and moon alignments. Some scholars suggest the underworld mentioned so often in the *Bible* and other ancient texts lies within the black hole of the Milky Way galaxy, which our sun aligns perfectly with on 12-21-12. Before drawing conclusions about UFOs and Christianity, let's examine the "last day" evidence to put that in better perspective.

Chapter 15:
THE UFO-LAST DAY CONNECTION

Consideration of the "last day" topic is relevant to our discussion here because ancient civilizations knew that a last day is coming sometime, and they reported obtained their information from sky people or the gods. These ancient people drew pictures and told stories of UFOs and many civilizations backed up their stories with incredible knowledge of the universe. The Maya in particular believed the last day would be 12-21-12.

The most recent "last day" was the day was the flood, likely 10,900 BC. Before that date, various ancient civilizations asserted that there were as many as five other "last days," such as the one sixty-five million years ago that killed off all the dinosaurs. There will definitely be another last day. The only thing debatable about that statement is when the last day will occur. The *Bible*, the *Popol Vuh*, the *Book of Enoch*, and other ancient writings confirm that a last day cataclysm will destroy the earth some time in the future.

Whenever a last day occurs, nearly all animals and plants will perish as occurred on all previous last days. *National Geographic* in 2008 reported that about 150,000 years ago the human species was reduced by a global catastrophe to about 2,000 individuals. Such events are why everyone worldwide is genetically very closely related. The flood around 10,900 BC reportedly reduced mankind from about 100 million people to 100,000. If another global catastrophe reduces mankind from about 7 billion people to a few million, that would be catastrophic, but definitely would not be the first time such an event has occurred.

According to ancient texts, on the last day, Jesus and God will return to earth with 20,000 UFOs and destroy the forces of Satan as well as sinners. For example, Isaiah 27:1 says, "In that day the LORD with his great and strong sword shall punish leviathan the piercing serpent, even leviathan that crooked serpent; and he shall slay the dragon that is in the sea."

But not everyone will perish on the last day, as indicated by Jesus who is quoted in Ezekiel (34:22-24) saying, "Therefore will I save my flock, and they shall no more be a prey; and I will judge between cattle. And I will set up one shepherd over them, and he shall feed them, my servant David; he shall feed them, and he shall be their shepherd. And I the LORD will be their God, and my servant David a prince among them; I the LORD have spoken it."

The Maya, Hopi Indians, the Chinese *Book of Changes* also believed the last day will be 12-21-12. The Mayan calendar ends at 6:12 a.m. on the East Coast of the USA on 12-21-12 when it reaches the end of a 394-year cycle called a baktun. This baktun is part of a larger 8,000-year cycle called a pictun. The current baktun slides into the next cycle on that date.

Unaware of the Mayan calendar's end date, Nahul-Ollin, Dennis and Terrence McKenna calculated the "end of time" from the Chinese ruler I Ching's Chinese *Book of Changes*. Written between 50 BC and 10 AD, the Chinese *Book of Changes* describes a system of hexagram symbols believed to discern order or patterns from past earthly events. The McKenna's 1975 book *The Invisible Landscape* pinpoints 12-21-12 as the end of time. That book preceded scholars' realization that the Mayan calendar predicts that same end date. The McKenna book does not mention the Maya at all.

The *India Times* (*http://www.indiadaily.com/editorial/1753.asp*) on March 1, 2005, described how geophysicists and astrophysicists anticipate that the earth and sun both will go through a process of magnetic pole reversal in 2012. Called the Hyderabad Computer Model, the article reported that the earth's magnetosphere will weaken as we approach that date and cosmic radiation from the sun will increase dramatically. A "geomagnetic reversal" is a change in the orientation of earth's magnetic field such that the positions of magnetic north and magnetic south become interchanged. Scientists now know that the earth's magnetic field has reversed its orientation hundreds and perhaps thousands of times since its formation several billion years ago. With the increasingly accurate Global Polarity Timescale (GPTS), it is now known that the rate at which reversals occur has varied widely in the past. During some periods of geologic time, the earth's magnetic field has maintained a single orientation for ten million years, but in one period of time two earth geomagnetic reversals occurred in a span of fifty thousand years.

The last pole reversal was the Brunhes-Matuyama reversal approximately 780,000 years ago. This reversal occurred over several thousand years. In 2006, a team of physicists at the University of Calabria discovered that the frequency of pole reversals conform to a Levy mathematical distribution. Some scientists assert that there is a direct causal relation between geomagnetic pole reversals and biological extinctions, including Florida State University professor David E. Loper. A pole shift could perhaps release Satan and his forces from the underworld to plague humanity.

In January 2009, geophysicists at the U.S. National Academy of Sciences announced that a super solar storm could catastrophically impact earth sometime in 2012, when sunspots will become especially numerous and active. Sunspots can be the size of the planet Jupiter and are concentrations of intense magnetic activity. Sunspots are basically planet-sized magnets that can have a dramatic impact on the earth's magnetic field. Sunspots also eject solar flares far into our solar system. These flares are thousands of miles long and are coronal masses of plasma. Once emitted, a solar flare reaches the earth in about eighteen hours. A 2008 NASA report called *Severe Space Weather Events: Understanding Societal and Economic Impacts* warns of "dramatic impact that extreme space weather can have on the technology of modern society." In 1989, millions in Canada were left without power for several hours when a solar storm wreaked havoc on northeastern Canada's Hydro-Quebec power grid.

Solar storms or flares can threaten modern infrastructure and even life itself according to Yousaf Butt, a physicist in the High-Energy Astrophysics Division at the Harvard-Smithsonian Center for Astrophysics. "It is virtually guaranteed that a powerful geomagnetic storm, capable of knocking out a significant section of the U.S. electrical grid, will occur within the next few decades," Butt wrote in *The Space Review*. "In fact, this may well happen within next few years as we approach the next period of elevated solar activity, ... which is forecast to peak in 2013." The peak of the next sunspot cycle is expected in late 2011 or mid-2012 — affecting airline flights, communications satellites and electrical transmissions. But forecasters disagree on how intense it will be, ranging from a moderately strong cycle of 140 sunspots expected to peak in October of 2011 to a moderately weak cycle of 90 sunspots peaking in August of 2012. A picture is given below of a solar flare.

A Solar Flare

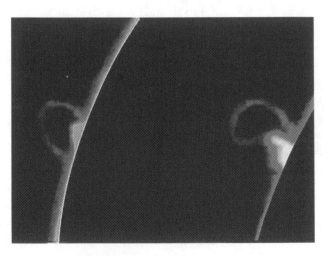

Source: *http://en.wikipedia.org/wiki/File:Flare_and_after-flare_prominence.jpg*

Every century or so, a ten-meter meteor impacts earth with the force of a small nuclear device. The last such meteor was in 1908 in Tunguska, an uninhabited wilderness area of Siberia. Luckily, the Tunguska meteor landed on barren land. Every few thousand years, our planet can pass through unusually thick parts of the debris trail of comets, turning the familiar light show of a meteor shower into a deadly firestorm. Roughly every one-hundred thousand years, a meteor or asteroid hundreds of meters across impacts earth and unleashes power equal to the world's nuclear arsenals. The result is devastation over an area the size of England, global tidal waves (if the impact is in the ocean), and enough dust flung into the atmosphere to dim the sun and kill off vegetation. About every one hundred million years, a larger asteroid slams into the earth, causing global earthquakes, mile-high tidal waves, and immediate death to all large land animals. Creatures in the sea soon follow, as trillions of tons of vaporized rock cause drastic cooling and the destruction of the food chain based on photosynthesis. Scientists are nearly certain this happened sixty-five million years ago, killing all the dinosaurs. A similar event may also have happened about 10,900 BC causing the flood.

The Maya (and maybe their Atlantis forebearers) astonishingly knew that on 12-21-12 our sun aligns perfectly with the galactic equator, which is the exact central line of the Milky Way galaxy. Astronomers today call this area of the Milky Way a black hole, which, according to the general theory of relativity, is a region of space from which nothing, including light, can escape. In 2008, astronomers found compelling evidence that the super massive black hole of more than four million solar masses is located near the Sagittarius A region in the center of the Milky Way. The 12-21-12 solar alignment is expected to cause a rift at the galactic core. This upcoming event at 6:12 a.m. Eastern Standard Time on 12-21-12 went undiscovered by modern science until the mid-1900s. It is a mystery how the Maya knew three thousand years ago about our sun's upcoming alignment with the black hole of the Milky Way.

Also on 12-21-12, our earth will "wobble" on its axis, which occurs only once every 25,800 years. Astronomers refer to this movement as "precession of the earth's axis of rotation" or "precession of the equinoxes." Like a wobbling top, the direction of the earth's axis changes constantly, but does a complete reversal every 25,800 years, which is set to occur on 12-21-12. Besides tectonic upheaval, a consequence of precession is a changing pole star. Currently Polaris in the sky marks the position of the north celestial pole, but in 3000 BC, Thuban in the constellation Draco, was the earth's North Pole star. The brilliant star named Vega in the constellation Lyra was the earth's North Pole star about 12,000 BC and will be again about 14,000 AD. This is all complicated astronomy requiring mathematical formulas, but the Maya miraculously knew the details long ago. They must have had high-tech alien assistance of some kind.

In 2008, Habibullah Abdusamatov, head of Russia's Pulkovo Observatory space research lab, told the RIA Novosti Press Agency that "earth has passed the peak of its warmer period, and a fairly cold spell will set in quite soon, by 2012. Real cold will come when solar activity reaches its minimum, by 2041." Many scientists worldwide now expect another abrupt ice age to begin very soon, despite the short-term global warming.

Even if scientists already know or soon determine that a last day is going to occur soon, this information clearly would be withheld from mankind to avert social and political panic. Perhaps in anticipation of such an event, Russia has built an underground survival complex to house sixty thousand of their people. This facility is named the Yamantau Mountain Complex and is located hundreds of miles directly east of Moscow at GPS 53.32.56 north / 58.34.57 east. A map of this location is given on the next page.

The Russian Yamantau Mountain Complex

Source: This picture is available a numerous Web sites, including:
http://www.wnd.com/?pageId=4137
http://viewzone2.com/yamantaux.html

Perhaps in anticipation of a "last day" event, the USA and NATO have jointly built and stocked a gigantic underground seed bank that houses seeds from almost every plant on earth. Named the Svalbard

Global Seed Vault, this facility is located on the Norwegian island of Spitsberger near the town of Longyearbyen in the remote Arctic Svalbard archipelago about 810 miles from the North Pole. A picture of the entrance to the facility is given below:

The Svalbard Global Seed Vault Near The North Pole

Source: *http://en.wikipedia.org/wiki/File:Svalbard_ Global_Seed_Vault_main_entrance_1.jpg*

Additional factual information regarding the upcoming 2012 winter solstice is provided at the following three Web sites:

http://www.youtube.com/watch?v=2ahoPGzL50Q&feature=related - A ten-minute documentary is provided by Brooks Agnew on the possible 12-21-12 North Pole to South Pole flip that could occur in seventy-two hours on earth around that date.

http://www.youtube.com/watch?v=wxQsLLOYC7Q&feature=related A ten-minute documentary is provided by Daniel Pinchbeck on the

Mayan 2012 calculation of the earth's alignment, precession, and pole shift.

http://www.youtube.com/watch?v=jT4hrd6To2k&NR=1 A ten-minute documentary is provided on Edgar Cayce's predictions regarding an upcoming Web sites earth pole shift.

When asked "do you know when the last day will occur?" Jesus is quoted in Matthew 24:35-36 saying, "Heaven and Earth will pass away, but my words shall not pass away. But of that day and hour, not even the angels of heaven, nor the Son, but the Father alone." Thus, Jesus did not know when the last day will occur and scientists today may or may not know. Many *Bible* verses speak about the last day in the context of a cloud, such as the following:

Luke 21: 25-32: There will be signs in the sun, moon, and stars. On the earth, nations will be in anguish and perplexity at the roaring and tossing of the sea. 26 Men will faint from terror, apprehensive of what is coming on the world, for the heavenly bodies will be shaken. 27 At that time they will see the Son of Man *coming in a cloud* with power and great glory. 28 When these things begin to take place, stand up and lift up your heads, because your redemption is drawing near." 29 He told them this parable: "Look at the fig tree and all the trees. 30 When they sprout leaves, you can see for yourselves and know that summer is near. 31 Even so, when you see these things happening, you know that the kingdom of God is near. 32 I tell you the truth, this generation will certainly not pass away until all these things have happened."

Matthew 24:30: "At that time the sign of the Son of Man will appear in the sky, and all the nations of the earth will mourn. They will see the Son of Man coming on *the clouds of the sky*, with power and great glory."

Acts 1:9-11: "After he said this, he was taken up before their very eyes, and a *cloud* hid him from their sight. 10 They were looking intently up into the sky as he was going, when suddenly two men dressed in white stood beside them. 11 "Men of Galilee," they said, "why do you stand here looking into the sky? This same Jesus, who has been taken from you into heaven, will *come back in the same way you have seen him go into heaven."*

In summary, ancient people witnessed, wrote, and told about obtaining knowledge from aliens who traveled in UFOs who enabled them to predict celestial events and align megalithic structures to planets and stars. This was an important part of the history of many early civilizations. There could be little to no warning of the last day, especially if a solar flare or pole reversal were to be the cause. Many scientists disregard both the 12-21-12 Mayan calendar's last day and the existence of UFOs, but there may indeed be signs in the sun, moon, and stars. Let's now examine in further detail whether the UFO-Christianity connection is fact or fiction.

Chapter 16:
THE UFO-CHRISTIANITY CONNECTION

From November 6 to 10 in 2008, the Vatican conducted a five-day astrobiology conference where scientists convened to discuss the acknowledgement and implications of extraterrestrial life. The conference primarily focused on detection of primitive extraterrestrial life forms, and featured presentations from nearly thirty international experts in astronomy, physics and biology. The conference's lead person was director of the Vatican Observatory, Jesuit priest Father Jose Gabriel Funes. Earlier in May 2008, Funes gave an interview to the Vatican's *L'Osservatore Romano* newspaper where he said, "The existence of intelligent extraterrestrials poses no problems to Catholic theology."

The Vatican's November 2008 conference was officially convened by the Vatican's Pontifical Academy of Sciences, chaired by its religious leader Bishop Marcelo Sanchez Sorondo, and held on private Vatican grounds. The conference revealed an openness by the Vatican to the possibility and implications of extraterrestrial life. This conference came on the heels of an openness policy adopted by the United Nations in February 2008. Apparently the Vatican (Catholic Church) is accelerating its Public Acclimation Program to assure its faithful, and anyone else who will listen, that star visitors (aliens in UFOs) are real, are in the *Bible*, and are children of God too. The Vatican's Monsignor Corrado Balducci died on September 20, 2008 in Italy, but soon before he passed away he proclaimed on Italian national television that encounters people have had and do have with star visitors are real, not a delusion, and not a case of demon possession. Balducci also said these star visitors appear to be more advanced, intellectually and spiritually, than humans.

The Vatican's Jesuit Brother Guy Consolmagno, an expert astronomer at the Vatican Observatory atop Mount Graham, Arizona, wrote in the April 2006 issue of *Harper's Magazine* the following, "There are, unquestionably, nonhuman intelligent beings in the *Bible*." He quoted Jesus as saying, "I have other sheep that do not belong to this fold." Then Consolmagno wrote, "And perhaps it's not so far-fetched to see the Second Person of the Trinity not only as the Son of Man but also as a Child of other races. Any creature in the universe, created and loved by the same God who created and loves us, ... Would they deserve to be called alien?" Then Consolmagno said, "God is bigger than whatever parallel universes may or may not exist beyond our own. And God is able to concentrate his entire effort, energy and love on each one of us tiny individuals on this tiny planet. And, I have confidence, on any other individuals on any other planet as well." Consolmagno is a Harvard and MIT trained with a Ph.D.

Transfiguration of Jesus

Numerous passages and incidents in the *Bible* suggest that God may travel the universe in a UFO and perhaps was on-site on earth during biblical days. For example, at the Transfiguration of Jesus on Mount Tabor, a cloud (UFO) came and overshadowed Jesus, Peter, James, and John, as described in Matthew 17:1-8 below. God the Father, along with Moses and Elijah, were in that cloud. God spoke from that cloud. The Church of the Transfiguration, pictured on the next page, is located today on Mount Tabor in Israel. Sometimes Mount Tabor is referred to as the Mount of Transfiguration.

Matthew 17: 1-8
1 Six days later Jesus took with Him Peter and James and John his brother, and led them up on a high mountain by themselves.
2 And He was transfigured before them; and His face shone like the sun, and His garments became as white as light.

3 And behold, Moses and Elijah appeared to them, talking with Him.

4 Peter said to Jesus, "Lord, it is good for us to be here; if You wish, I will make three tabernacles here, one for You, and one for Moses, and one for Elijah."

5 While he was still speaking, a bright cloud overshadowed them, and behold, a voice out of the cloud said, "This is My beloved Son, with whom I am well-pleased; listen to Him!"

6 When the disciples heard this, they fell face down to the ground and were terrified.

7 And Jesus came to them and touched them and said, "Get up, and do not be afraid."

8 And lifting up their eyes, they saw no one except Jesus Himself alone.

Mount Tabor in Israel: Site of the Transfiguration of Jesus

Source: *http://en.wikipedia.org/wiki/
File:Mount_of_transfiguration_is.JPG*

The Baptism of Jesus

When John the Baptist baptized Jesus in the Jordan River, Jesus then began his public ministry. Jesus' baptism is recorded in the *Bible* in Matthew, Mark, Luke, and in Acts 19:1-7. Even when Jesus was a child, John the Baptist preached that baptism was required for forgiveness of sins and he baptized many people in the Jordan River. John the Baptist baptized Jesus at a site traditionally known as Qasr at-Yahud. Ancient writings say the event concluded with the heavens opening, a dove-like descent of the Holy Spirit, and a voice from a cloud saying: "This is my beloved Son with whom I am well pleased."

A famous *"Baptism of Christ"* painting was completed in 1475 by Italian Renaissance painter Andrea del Verrocchio and Leonardo da Vinci. This painting hangs today in the Uffizi Gallery in Florence, Italy and may be viewed online at *http://en.wikipedia.org/wiki/File:Andrea_del_Verrocchio_002.jpg*

Another famous painting, pictured below, is titled *"The Baptism of Christ"* and hangs on the wall in the Fitzwilliam Museum in Cambridge, England. This painting was completed in 1710 by Dutch artist Aert De Gelder. As provided on the next page, note in the painting that a UFO is shining beams of light on John the Baptist and Jesus.

Note that the white circular UFO depicted in Aert De Gelder's famous *"The Baptism of Christ"* painting is quite similar to pictures taken on July 7, 2010 of the UFO in China. As mentioned earlier in this book, on the night of July 7, 2010, a UFO flew into the airspace of the Xiaoshan Airport near Hangzhou, the capital of east China's Zhejiang Province. The airport closed all flights in and out from 9:00 p.m. to 10:00 p.m. as the UFO was tracked on radar. Around 1:00 a.m. that evening, just after the airport had reopened, Hangzhou residents reported seeing a large, brightly lit UFO in the sky. Two pictures of the recent UFO over China are provided on the next two pages.

"The Baptism of Christ" – A 1710 Painting by Aert De Gelder

Source: This is a public domain picture available at many sites, including: *http://en.wikipedia.org/wiki/File:BaptismO fChristByAertDeGelder_Fitzwilliam_Cambridge.jpg*

July 7, 2010 – UFO in China (pic1)

Source: This is a public domain picture available at many sites, including: *http://www.csmonitor.com/Science/Discoveries/2010/0716/ UFO-over-Chinese-airport-VIDEO*

July 7, 2010 - UFO in China (pic2)

Source: This is a public domain picture
available at many sites, including:
http://www.bing.com/videos/?FORM=MFEVID&publ=DCD
*0EAAB-C0E7-4508-A3A642EAED4340AE&crea=STND_*
MFEVID_core_HuffPoQ1FY11_CustomVidLink_1x1&q=China
+UFO+Sightings&docid=182718628593&FORM=HUFPST

A video made of the July 7, 2010 UFO in China may be seen at this Web site *http://www.youtube.com/watch?v=A-h7DaJCqx4*

The Annunciation

As described in Luke 1:26-38, the "Annunciation" refers to an event when God sent archangel Gabriel to inform Virgin Mary that she had been chosen to conceive and give birth to the Son of God - Jesus. Ancient writings indicate that Mary, the mother of Jesus, was a scholar, which was a bit unusual for women in biblical times. When Gabriel made his announcement, Mary was perhaps reading a book in a study as depicted in two famous paintings given on the next two pages.

The first painting, titled *"The Annunciation,"* was completed by Carlo Crivelli in 1486. The painting is on display in the National Gallery in London. Notice that a UFO is shining a beam of light through the house wall and down onto the top of Mary's head.

"*The Annunciation*" – A 1486 AD Painting by Carlo Crivelli

Source: This is a public domain picture at many Web sites including: *http://en.wikipedia.org/wiki/Carlo_Crivelli*

The second painting is by the Netherlandish master artist Jan van Eyck and was completed in 1434. Titled "*The Annunciation*," this famous oil painting hangs today in the National Gallery of Art in Washington, DC. This picture shows seven rays of light, presumably from a UFO, coming through the upper window to the left, with a dove symbolizing the Holy Spirit following the same path. Biblical scholars believe this is the moment when God's plan for salvation is set in motion, with the old era of the Law being transformed into the new era of Grace. The inscription of this painting shows Archangel Gabriel's words "AVE GRÁ. PLENA" or "Hail, full of grace." Mary modestly draws back and responds, "ECCE ANCILLA DÑI." or "Behold the handmaiden of the Lord." Her words are painted upside down for God above to see.

"*The Annunciation*" – A 1434 AD Painting by Jan van Eyck

Source of Picture 37 Below
http://en.wikipedia.org/wiki/File:Annunciation_-_
Jan_van_Eyck_-_1434_-_NG_Wash_DC.jpg

God seems to acknowledge in the *Bible* that he is the Father over a family or council of gods or twelve archangels. This interpretation would be consistent with the writings from virtually all ancient civilizations that refer to gods in the plural. The *Quran* too refers to God in the plural.

Genesis 1:26 says, "And God said, *Let us make man in our image, after our likeness*; and let him have dominion over the fish of the sea, and over the fowl of the air, and over the cattle, and over all the earth, and over every creeping thing that creepth upon the earth."

Psalm 89:6-8: "For who in the skies can be compared to the Lord? Who among the heavenly beings is like the Lord, a God feared in the council of the hold ones, great and terrible above all that are round about him? O lord God of hosts, who is might as thou art, O Lord, with thy faithfulness round about thee?"

Psalm 82:1 God presides in the great assembly; he gives judgment among the "gods." (6) I said, You are "gods"; you are all sons of the Most High. (7) But you will die like mere men; and will fall like every other ruler."

Most traditional Christian faiths today, however, profess that there is only one God and that the word "our" in Genesis 1:26 for example refers to the trinity. Perhaps there is only one God the Father, but he likely is at the head of the table, presiding over an assembly or council of at least twelve archangels. Most ancient civilizations such as the Egyptians believed there was a family of twelve important gods. Of course there were twelve tribes of Israel and Jesus had twelve disciples. Twelve was an important number in antiquity. It is ironic that the date 12-21-12 includes the number twelve.

It is likely that ancient aliens came to earth perhaps as far back as one million years ago and dramatically altered the evolution of man. God the Father may have been responsible for this intervention, but the evidence suggests that fallen angels were working against God's will. The human DNA was unraveled in 1953 by Francis Crik who postulated that mankind originated most likely from some celestial body somewhere in the universe. He said we are descendants from an alien race and suggested that we are colonists from another world.

Genetic evidence for alien intervention in human evolution was discovered in 2003 when geneticists discovered the HARI gene among the 23,000 genes in the human genome. The HARI gene is unique to humans and sets us apart from all other animals. Scientists are unsure where that gene came from. Francis Crik says the HARI gene could not have evolved from lower forms of life on earth and was thus inserted into the human genome on purpose by God. Anthropologists therefore likely have the human evolution story all right, except for the divine intervention that occurred sometime in our distant past. That divine intervention makes people exponentially more advanced than chimpanzees or dolphin. We are not the product only of evolution. Prehistoric man was purposely altered by fallen angels or God, as recorded in many ancient writings.

There is just no way that prehistoric civilizations independent of each other all over the planet fabricated all the stories, pictures, and writings of ancient aliens and UFOs. The Native Americans for example welcomed early explorers everywhere - in North America, Central America, and South America - all believing the explorers were the same sky gods described in stories and pictures passed down from their ancestors hundreds and thousands of years earlier. There is just no way either that the Maya could have known about celestial events to occur 12-21-12, or that the Egyptians could have built the Great Pyramid of Giza, without ancient alien assistance. The strength and validity of the UFO connection to ancient civilizations adds credence to the UFO-Christianity connection.

We may never know for sure until the end of time whether the UFO-Christianity connection is fact or fiction, but this book provides a basis for readers to decide for themselves. The Vatican, United Nations, and many scholars are moving towards accepting the connection as fact. But many people still contend the connection is fiction. The evidence across time, distance, and discipline however suggests that the UFO-Christianity relationship is fact, not fiction. Countless witnesses, stories, pictures, and ancient writings, including the *Bible*, provide a basis for this conclusion. It may not be politically correct or easy for some persons to acknowledge that God the Father, Jesus and watchers, as well as fallen angels, Satan, and other alien beings elsewhere in the universe may all travel in UFOs.

Presumably today, any UFOs that fallen angels or Satan retain are generally confined to the underworld, whereas God's watchers or guardian angels freely traverse between the earth and moon, which may be their home base or spaceport. It is human nature to resist changing in a basic belief. Quite often in history however, a change in beliefs has been the right thing, even if the face of disagreement. Even Christianity for centuries persecuted non-believers, endorsed slavery, and held women in very low esteem, but we all know today those beliefs are wrong. Many people disagreed with Jesus during his days on earth simply because of their resistance to change. Being politically correct is obviously not always the right thing to do.

With the Vatican and new discoveries daily paving the way as well as more governmental disclosure, sooner or later, the truth regarding UFOs will become apparent. Millions of ancient people for thousands of years based their whole belief system on alien visitation of gods physically coming to earth in UFOs. From the biblical wise men to the Hopi Indians, our forebears on all continents did all they could in pictures, stories, carvings, sculptures, and writings to pass down to us the truth about ancient aliens. Most *Bible* stories already have been or likely will be corroborated by ancient writings, stories, pictures, and archaeological finds. The UFO connection with the *Bible* was shown to be quite clear, and even clearer with the Hindu *Vedas, Book of Enoch, Popul Vuh*, and other ancient writings.

During biblical times from say about 2000 BC to 400 AD, God the Father was present in "clouds and chariots" and responsible for many of the events in the *Bible*. It is admirable to accept biblical stories by *blind faith* – such as the Flood, Tower of Babel, Garden of Eden, Jonah and the whale, parting of the Red Sea, virgin birth, miracles that Jesus performed, and the resurrection. However, in addition to *blind faith*, this book provides a scientific basis for the realization that most if not all events described in the *Bible* indeed happened, some perhaps because God was onsite in a UFO. God's watchers may use UFOs even today to monitor humanity as guardian angels. Perhaps they use our moon as their home base. God's watchers today could be responsible for such activities as: (1) answering prayers, (2) performing miracles, (3) managing souls as people die, (4) making sure Satan and the underworld remain in check, (5) keeping God and Jesus informed, and (6) monitoring or influencing world events.

UFOs may actually be the missing link between science and religion. Hopefully this book interests you to examine further the evidence for UFOs across discipline, distance, and time to gain a better understanding of the connection between science and religion. These two bodies of knowledge are actually much more closely related than most people realize. The *Bible* reveals that God actually expects mankind to think scientifically; to strive to become all that he or she can become, as indicated in Romans 12:2, which says: "And be not conformed to this world: but be ye transformed by the renewing of your mind, that ye may prove what is that good, and acceptable, and perfect, will of God." Therefore, by expanding one's knowledge base, even of the UFO-Christianity connection as provided in this book, a person may become a better witness for whatever they believe.

The clear UFO connection with the Maya, Aztec, Sumerians, Indians, Atlanteans, Enoch, the Flood, giants, the Sons of God, and the last day is apparent. Like *Chariots of the Gods*, this book for many people reinforces that the *Bible* is the gospel. This book may strengthen your belief that Jesus "was who he said he was" and that we are "not alone in the universe." For Eric Von Daniken and I and hopefully you, exploring the UFO-Christianity connection in greater detail leads to a better understanding of the past, present, and future.

A primary conclusion from the evidence is that Jesus ascended into a UFO both at the Transfiguration and the Resurrection, and will return on the last day with 20,000 UFOs. I believe that is fact rather than fiction, but thank goodness in America and many places in the world today, people are free to study the evidence, draw their own conclusions, and have faith in whomever or whatever they choose. Hopefully this book launches that exploration process for you, regardless of your faith or nationality.

No one is certain what Jesus actually looked like, but a common depiction from historical records and ancient paintings is provided on the next page.

A Painting of Jesus Completed About 526 AD and Located Today
at the Basilica of Saint'Appollinare Nuovo in Ravenna, Italy

Source:
http://upload.wikimedia.org/wikipedia/commons/c/
c9/Christus_Ravenna_Mosaic.jpg

Bibliography

Avasthi, Amitabh, "After Near Extinction, Humans Split Into Isolated Groups," *National*

Geographic, News, 24 April 2008, http://news.nationalgeographic.com/news/2008/04/08042/humans-extinct.html.

Bible

Book of Enoch

Chitty, John E.. *The Broken Bible: Picking Up The Extraterrestrial Pieces.* Lincoln, Nebraska: Writers' Club Press 2002.

Codex Vaticanus

Cooke, Patrick. *The Greatest Deception: The Bible UFO Connection.* Berkeley,

California: Oracle Research Publishing, 2004.

Dead Sea Scrolls

Epic of Gilgamesh

Frissell, Bob. *Nothing in this Book is True. But It's Exactly How Things Are.* Berkeley, California: Frog Books, 2009.

Hawking, Stephen and Mlodinow, Leonard, "Why God Did Not Create the Universe,"

Wall Street Journal, September 4-5, 2010, p. W3.

Joseph, Frank. *The Atlantis Encyclopedia*. Franklin Lakes, New Jersey: The Career Press 2005.

Joseph, Frank. *Atlantis and 2012*. Rochester, Vermont: Bear & Company, 2010.

Knight, Christopher and Butler, Alan. *Before the Pyramids: Cracking Archaeology's*

Greatest Mystery. London, England: Watkins Publishing, 2009.

Lloyd, Ellen. *Voices from Legendary Times*. Lincoln, Nebraska: iUniverse Books, 2005.

Malkowski, Edward F. *Sons of God: Daughters of Men*. Champaign, Illinois: Bits of Sunshine Publishing Company 2004.

Noorbergen, Rene. *Secrets of the Lost Races*. New York, New York: Teach Services, Inc., 2006.

Popol Vuh

Quran

Sitchin, Zecharia. *The Lost Realms*. New York, New York: HarperCollins Publishers, 2007.

Sitchin, Zecharia. *The 12th Planet*. New York, New York: HarperCollins Publishers, 2007.

Vedas

Von Daniken, Erich. *Chariots of the Gods*. New York, New York: Berkley Publishing Group, 1968.

YouTube Documentaries Related to This Book

http://www.youtube.com/watch?v=-gO4aYKVkB8
A four-minute video where American astronauts and Stephen Bassett discuss the truth regarding UFOs and their contact with people and governments.

http://www.youtube.com/watch?v=NCKoQ6FWyM4
A ten-minute video where Steven Greer, an American physician, author, lecturer and founder of the Orion Project and The Disclosure Project, introduces twenty different NASA, CIA, Army, Navy, and Air Force experts who give testimony regarding the presence of extraterrestrials on earth and the alleged government cover-up.

http://video.google.com/videoplay?docid=6552475158249898710#
A fifty-nine minute video reveals extensive testimony by experts describing classified UFO information.

http://www.dailyfinance.com/story/ufos-over-china-alien-invasion-or-economic-indicator/19559850/?icid=main|main|dl2|link4|http%3A%2F%2Fwww.dailyfinance.com%2Fstory%2Fufos-over-china-alien-invasion-or-economic-indicator%2F19559850%2F
A three-minute video shot on July 7, 2010, of a UFO in the sky near Xiaoshan airport in Hangzhou, a city outside Shanghai. See full article at http://srph.it/9rDv3c.

http://www.youtube.com/watch?v=wHqxlj_n-nk
A twenty-eight minute video where the director of the Vatican Observatory, George Coyne, discusses the purpose of the Observatory and the nature of science and religion. He has a PhD in Astronomy and is a Catholic priest.

http://www.youtube.com/watch?v=-nNZOjDi_dQ&feature=related
A thirty-five minute video where Rhawn Joseph, Ph.D, discusses scientific evidence for the Great Flood about 10900 BC and its impact on life.

http://www.youtube.com/watch?v=lAQhpwoH3c8
A three-minute, narrated tour of Lake Titicaca (on the border of Peru and Bolivia) and the Inca civilization.

http://www.youtube.com/watch?v=P2YBVlgqqco&NR=1&feature=f
vwp
A three-minute video where Michael Palin provides a narrated tour of Machu Picchu in Peru and the Inca civilization.

http://www.youtube.com/watch?v=3lGN5iq9azU&NR=1
A ten-minute video where Dr. Michael Zimmerman provides a documentary on Sumerian gods, and evidence for ancient alien visitation on earth. He talks about god genetic engineering man for the purpose of being primitive workers.

http://www.youtube.com/watch?v=D6wI3Pbolbw&feature=related
A three-minute documentary on the Mayan 12-21-12 last day of their calendar.

http://www.youtube.com/watch?v=2ahoPGzL50Q&feature=related
A ten-minute documentary by Brooks Agnew on the possible 12-21-12 North Pole to South Pole flip that could occur in seventy-two hours on earth around that date.

http://www.youtube.com/watch?v=wxQsLLOYC7Q&feature=related
A ten-minute documentary by Daniel Pinchbeck on the Mayan 2012 calculation of the earth's alignment, precession, and pole shift.

http://www.youtube.com/watch?v=jT4hrd6To2k&NR=1
A ten-minute documentary on Edgar Cayce's predictions regarding an upcoming earth pole shift.

http://www.youtube.com/watch?v=kTEOM_ZzKKk&feature=related
A ten-minute documentary on Atlantis.

http://www.youtube.com/watch?v=18CY7ZaCfzY&feature=related
A ten-minute documentary on the biblical and archeological evidence for giants.

http://www.youtube.com/watch?v=B-8bVEIVUh8&feature=related
A three-minute pictorial of skeletons of giant humans discovered at various places around the world.

http://www.youtube.com/watch?v=x2qaZFC2PtM&NR=1
Former NASA employees describe UFO moon bases.

http://www.youtube.com/watch?v=XlkV1ybBnHI&NR=1
Buzz Aldrin explains how a UFO traveled beside Apollo 11 on its way to the moon.

http://www.youtube.com/watch?v=bDIXvpjnRws&feature=related
Buzz Aldrin reveals there is a "god made" structure on a moon of Mars. He says "the universe put it there, or if you choose, god put it there," referring to an alien built structure.

http://www.youtube.com/watch?v=DplDreUFcEM&feature=related
Neil Armstrong tells kids on the 25th anniversary of that first moon landing, "there are great breakthroughs for those who can remove truths protective layers" – perhaps referring to a NASA cover-up.

http://www.youtube.com/watch?v=iSPQTfp5vJE&feature=related
A National Geographic documentary on the Apollo 11 moon landing.

History Channel Ten-Minute Segments on Ancient Aliens

http://www.youtube.com/watch?v=8DCCXbWTQNw
http://www.youtube.com/watch?v=E3y5h24sWuw
http://www.youtube.com/watch?v=2I5WSOseAvs&feature=related
http://www.youtube.com/watch?v=GvU1fuOkOHg&NR=1&feature=fvwp
http://www.youtube.com/watch?v=mCL2rhDjqD4&feature=related
http://www.youtube.com/watch?v=_7C6HydJhX8&feature=related
http://www.youtube.com/watch?v=iB0w7-Ft51Q&feature=related

http://www.youtube.com/watch?v=2Yl66RZ10qI&feature=related
http://www.youtube.com/watch?v=YSb29EWN4vo&feature=related
http://www.youtube.com/watch?v=MyLbcew-WMU&feature=related
http://www.youtube.com/watch?v=f9zKZ9HB9mQ&feature=related
http://www.youtube.com/watch?v=tgf5ahyf10s&feature=related
http://www.youtube.com/watch?v=zgbOOjjBOJk&feature=related
http://www.ufo-blogger.com/2009/05/history-channel-ufo-hunters-navy.html

Attribution for Pictures in this Book

Picture 1 - Front cover: *The Madonna with Saint Giovannino*
This is a public domain picture available at many Web sites. Nick
Hempsey designed the front cover from the famous painting named.
However, I emailed a request for permission to: Iconoclastpress3@
yahoo.com at the following Web site: http://www.cosmicchrist.net/
Christian_art_UFO_pictures_aliens_Jesus_Christ_Mary.htm
http://www.cosmicchrist.net/index.htm

Other sites where this front cover center painting appears include the
following:
1)   http://www.google.com/imgres?imgurl=http://asusta2.com.ar/
wp-content/uploads/2008/08/la-madonna-y-saint-giovannino.
jpg&imgrefurl=http://asusta2.com.ar/category/historia/page/17/&h=6
59&w=480&sz=112&tbnid=BBnVp1YKsTU3gM:&tbnh=263&tbnw
=192&prev=/images%3Fq%3DMadonna%2Bwith%2BSaint%2BGio
vannino&hl=en&usg=__cBudXb3RvV4FhMy6xbFN4OKsoEw=&sa
=X&ei=rPtKTIemG8L38Ab-wO02&ved=0CBkQ9QEwAA
2)   http://www.google.com/imgres?imgurl=http://bp1.blogger.com/_
STbd01ANT2w/RyzmIK1_HxI/AAAAAAAAADw/SRUSD5SrxHI/
S660/maryufoclose.jpg&imgrefurl=http://cosmicvisits.blogspot.
com/2007/11/northern-lights.html&h=296&w=622&sz=36&tbnid=
4QT_wXYEwfqoOM:&tbnh=65&tbnw=136&prev=/images%3Fq%
3DMadonna%2Bwith%2BSaint%2BGiovannino&hl=en&usg=__w
An51zOj5sTyv70pwksXXAzuqNw=&sa=X&ei=rPtKTIemG8L38Ab-
wO02&ved=0CBsQ9QEwAQ
3)   http://www.google.com/imgres?imgurl=http://xtctattoo.us/
ufo_Madonna-SaintGiovannino.jpg&imgrefurl=http://xtctattoo.us/
pastphoto.htm&h=560&w=365&sz=95&tbnid=sHD0CpF8S1ifX
M:&tbnh=133&tbnw=87&prev=/images%3Fq%3DMadonna%2B

with%2BSaint%2BGiovannino&hl=en&usg=__wmnFhb2ULhg-
Zf_AnvQKGVmYP_w=&sa=X&ei=rPtKTIemG8L38Ab-
wO02&ved=0CCEQ9QEwBA
4) http://terrifyingtales.blogspot.com/2007_01_01_archive.html
5) http://www.google.com/imgres?imgurl=http://bp3.blogger.com/_
vlhCksMUrhM/RkU_9cz3B5I/AAAAAAAAACU/7HvFzJO8gCg/
s400/Madonna_PVecchio.jpg&imgrefurl=http://medicinemonkey.
blogspot.com/2007/05/blog-post.html&h=400&w=400&sz=47&tb
nid=Eirifk-cYDfe_M:&tbnh=124&tbnw=124&prev=/images%3Fq%
3DMadonna%2Bwith%2BSaint%2BGiovannino&hl=en&usg=__t
VHIdt4rEpj1dttTTVau7zZHiq4=&sa=X&ei=rPtKTIemG8L38Ab-
wO02&ved=0CCcQ9QEwBw
6) http://asusta2.com.ar/wp-content/uploads/2008/08/la-madonna-y-
saint-giovannino.jpg
7)   http://www.thehistorybluff.com/wpcontent/uploads/2009/10/
madonna.jpg

Picture 2 - Of the Author
www.checkmateplan.com
www.prenhall.com/david
www.oceanislehistory.com

Picture 3 - UFO in Wales Picture
http://mathildasweirdworldweblog.wordpress.com/2008/06/22/welsh-
ufo-flap-in-progress/
http://mathildasweirdworldweblog.wordpress.com/
about/#comment-165

Picture 4 - Two Images of UFOs
   a. Sheffield, England, March 4, 1962
   b. Minneapolis, Minnesota, October 20, 1960
Two images of UFOs taken from http://en.wikipedia.org/wiki/File:P70.
gif
https://www.cia.gov/cgi-bin/comment_form.cgi and the CIA website
Page: (https://www.cia.gov/library/center-for-the-study-of-intelligence/
csi-publications/csi-studies/studies/97unclass/ufo.html)   Image:
(https://www.cia.gov/library/center-for-the-study-of-intelligence/csi-
publications/csi-studies/studies/97unclass/p70.gif)

Note: Wikipedia says this image is a work of a CIA employee, taken or made during the course of an employee's official duties. As a work of the U.S. federal government, the image is in the public domain. I emailed the CIA a permission request on July 20, 2010 at 6:00 p.m.
Picture 5 - Vatican Observatory Picture
http://en.wikipedia.org/wiki/Vatican_Observatory

Picture 6 – Historians' Depiction of the Exodus Route
http://en.wikipedia.org/wiki/File:Exodus_Map.jpg
The map was generated based on an image from http://www.planiglobe.com
Routes drawn by ThaThinker.

Picture 7 – Jacob's Ladder as Described in Genesis 28:10-22
http://en.wikipedia.org/wiki/File:JacobsLaddertoHeaven.jpg
Original source: *Standard Bible Story Readers, Book Three* with authors O.A. Stemler and Bess Bruce Cleveland.

Picture 8 – The Great Pyramid of Giza
Source: http://upload.wikimedia.org/wikipedia/commons/e/e3/Kheops-Pyramid.jpg
This picture was taken by Nina Aldin Thune in the immediate vicinity of the image.

Picture 9 – The Great Sphinx at Giza
http://en.wikipedia.org/wiki/File:Great_Sphinx_of_Giza_-_20080716a.jpg
This picture was taken on July 16, 2008 by Paul Solomon.

Picture 10 – Ancient Map of Sumeria
http://history-world.org/Sumer-Akkad.jpg
This picture was originally uploaded by John D. Croft.

Picture 11 – Common Depiction of a Neanderthal Male's Profile
http://en.wikipedia.org/wiki/File:Neanderthaler_Fund.png
This picture was originally developed by Hermann Schaaffhausen associated with Ther Neanderthaler Fund published by Marcus, Bonn

Picture 12 – Comparing a Neanderthal Skull with a Human Skull
http://en.wikipedia.org/wiki/File:Neandertal_vs_Sapiens.jpg

Picture 13 – Cuzco, Peru As It Looks Today
http://en.wikipedia.org/wiki/File:Cuscoinfobox.png
This picture was developed by montage was developed by Vivaperucarajo on December 12, 2008 but the photos were taken by Christophe Meneboeuf, Hakan Svensson, Colegota, and Thomas Quine.

Picture 14 – Lake Titicaca Map
http://en.wikipedia.org/wiki/File:Lake_Titicaca_map.png
This map originally appeared at http://www.aquarius.geomar.de/omc/

Picture 15 – Nazca Drawing of a Monkey
http://en.wikipedia.org/wiki/File:Nazca_monkey.jpg
This picture was taken by Maria Reiche in 1953 and originally owned by her family Walter Humala.

Picture 16 - The Olmec Empire
http://en.wikipedia.org/wiki/File:Formative_Era_sites.svg

Picture 17 – Stonehenge in England as It Looked in 1649
http://upload.wikimedia.org/wikipedia/commons/2/2e/Stonehenge_-_Wiltonia_sive_Comitatus_Wiltoniensis%3B_Anglice_Wilshire_%28Atlas_van_Loon%29.jpg
The source of this picture is Atlas van Loon but the author is unknown.

Picture 18 – Megalithic Statues on Easter Island in the South Pacific
http://en.wikipedia.org/wiki/File:Ahu-Akivi-1.JPG
This photo was taken by Ian Sewell in July 2006 and originally was shown at http://www.ianandwendy.com/OtherTrips/SouthPacific/Easter-Island/index.htm

Picture 19 - A Map of the Aztec Empire in the Year 1519
http://en.wikipedia.org/wiki/File:Aztec_Empire_1519_map-fr.svg

This image is a derivative work of several images as listed at the Web site.

Picture 20 - Mayan Temple at Chichen Itza
http://en.wikipedia.org/wiki/File:Chichen-Itza-Castillo-Seen-From-East.JPG
This picture was taken on June 10, 2007 by Bjorn Christian Torrissen and originally seen at http://bjornfree.com/galleries.html

Picture 21 – The Ancient Indus Valley Region in India
http://en.wikipedia.org/wiki/File:CiviltàValleIndoMappa.png

Picture 22 – The Mayan Long Count Calendar
This picture is in the public domain viewable at many web sites, including
(1) http://www.google.com/imgres?imgurl=http://jonathanephraim.files.wordpress.com/2008/07/mayancalendar.jpg&imgrefurl=http://jonathanephraim.wordpress.com/2008/07/24/12-21-12/&h=420&w=419&sz=132&tbnid=p-6k2r7loIMcUM:&tbnh=125&tbnw=125&prev=/images%3Fq%3Dmayan%2Blong%2Bcount%2Bcalendar&hl=en&usg=__ttMg38F6H8gNMGEtkezgR_cpDQQ=&sa=X&ei=yTpKTK7UNYK88gb3w-E0&ved=0CDQQ9QEwBg and
(2)
http://www.google.com/imgres?imgurl=http://i185.photobucket.com/albums/x271/DukeBuzzy/MayanCalendar.jpg&imgrefurl=http://picsdigger.com/keyword/mayan%2520long%2520count%2520calendar/&h=432&w=432&sz=207&tbnid=1eLTEuYh4mIDsM:&tbnh=126&tbnw=126&prev=/images%3Fq%3Dmayan%2Blong%2Bcount%2Bcalendar&hl=en&usg=__Rl0GpwNFrEBw9ix2tTiqB8k7Big=&sa=X&ei=xhQ9TKGyEIG88ga4msDUDg&ved=0CDcQ9QEwBA

Picture 23 – A Picture of Edgar Cayce in 1910
http://en.wikipedia.org/wiki/File:Cayce_1910.jpg
This picture first appeared on the front page of *The New York Times* prior to January 1, 1923.

Picture 24 – A Picture of Plato

http://en.wikipedia.org/wiki/File:Plato-raphael.jpg
This is a faithful photographic reproduction of an original two-dimensional work of art done in 1520 by Italian painter and architect Raffaello Sanzio (1483-1520).

Picture 25 - Map of Lemuria and Atlantis
http://en.wikipedia.org/wiki/File:Book_map1.jpg
Map from "The Lost Continent of Mu," (1927) by James Churchward and originally seen at http://www.my-mu.com/mapgallery.html

Picture 26 – A Mammoth Life-Size Reconstruction
http://upload.wikimedia.org/wikipedia/commons/9/9c/Mammoth_Mammut_model.JPG
The author of this picture, taken at Kirchberg (Tyrol), Austria. is Titus322. Originally created on September 24, 2009.

Picture 27 – Giant Human Femur
www.mtblanco.com
E-mail from director Joe Taylor of the Mt. Blanco Museum granting permission. Cost of permission was $10, paid by check.

Picture 28 – Color-Coded North America Map of Bigfoot Sightings
http://en.wikipedia.org/wiki/Bigfoot
The author of this is Fiziker but the information was created on September 8, 2008 as adapted from the BFRO Geographical Database at http://www.bfro.net/GDB/

Picture 29 – A Solar Flare
http://en.wikipedia.org/wiki/File:Flare_and_after-flare_prominence.jpg
Originally created by Mila at http://home.comcast.net/~milazinkova/Fogshadow.html

Picture 30 - The Russian Yamantau Mountain Complex
This is a public domain picture that is available on numerous Web sites, including: http://www.wnd.com/?pageId=4137
http://viewzone2.com/yamantaux.html

Picture 31 - The Svalbard Global Seed Vault Near the North Pole
http://en.wikipedia.org/wiki/File:Svalbard_Global_Seed_Vault_main_entrance_1.jpg
The author of this image is Mari Tefre who took this picture on February 26, 2008.

Picture 32 - Mount Tabor
http://en.wikipedia.org/wiki/File:Mount_of_transfiguration_is.JPG
This picture was taken in Palestine in 2005 by Bantosh.

Picture 33 - *"The Baptism of Christ"* – A 1710 Painting by Aert De Gelder
This is a public domain picture available at many sites, including:
(1) http://en.wikipedia.org/wiki/File:BaptismOfChristByAertDeGelder_Fitzwilliam_Cambridge.jpg
(2) http://www.cosmicchrist.net/Christian_art_UFO_pictures_aliens_Jesus_Christ_Mary.htm
(3) http://lithiumdreamer.tripod.com/ufoart.html
(4) http://www.karenlyster.com/jesusufo.html

Picture 34 – July 2010 China UFO (pic1)
This is a public domain picture available at many sites, including:
(1) http://www.csmonitor.com/Science/Discoveries/2010/0716/UFO-over-Chinese-airport-VIDEO
(2) http://stupidcelebrities.net/2010/07/15/china-ufo-ufo-over-china-2010-photos-videos/

Picture 35 – July 2010 China UFO (pic2)
This is a public domain picture available at many sites, including:

(1) http://www.bing.com/videos/?FORM=MFEVID&publ=DCD0EAAB-C0E7-4508-A3A642EAED4340AE&crea=STND_MFEVID_core_HuffPoQ1FY11_CustomVidLink_1x1&q=China+UFO+Sightings&docid=182718628593&FORM=HUFPST

(2) http://news.lalate.com/2010/07/15/china-ufo-ufo-over-chinese-airport-2010-explained/

(3) http://stupidcelebrities.net/2010/07/15/china-ufo-ufo-over-china-2010-photos-videos/

Picture 36 - "*The Annunciation*" – A 1486 AD Painting by Carlo Crivelli
This is a public domain picture at many web sites including:
(1) http://en.wikipedia.org/wiki/Carlo_Crivelli
(2) http://www.nationalgallery.org.uk/paintings/carlo-crivelli-the-annunciation-with-saint-emidius
(3) http://lithiumdreamer.tripod.com/ufoart.html
(4) http://www.cosmicchrist.net/Christian_art_UFO_pictures_aliens_Jesus_Christ_Mary.htm

Picture 37 - "*The Annunciation*" – A 1434 AD Painting by Jan van Eyck
http://en.wikipedia.org/wiki/File:Annunciation_-_Jan_van_Eyck_-_1434_-_NG_Wash_DC.jpg

Picture 38 - Commonly Accepted Depiction of Jesus Christ
http://en.wikipedia.org/wiki/File:Christus_Ravenna_Mosaic.jpg
The original author of this was Aiden. Later versions were uploaded by Bilanovic, Gogo Dodo. This is a painting of Jesus located at the "Basilica of Saint'Apollinare Nuovo" in Ravenna, Italy: *Christ Surrounded By Angels and Saints*. A Mosaic of a Ravennate Italian-Byzantine Workshop, (Completed about 526 AD by the "Master of Saint'Apollinare").

Index

Abdel Rahman El-Aydi, 29

Abdusamatov, Habibullah, 96

Abominable Snowman, 80

Abyssinia, Ethiopia, 23

Acts, 15-16, 104

Adam and Eve, 22, 23, 35

Adapa, 34

Albright, William, 20

Aldrin, Buzz Jr., 86-87, 119

Alice P. Lennon Telescope, 12

Ambrose of Milan, 23

Amos, 13, 14, 19

Anakim, 77

Andhakas, 60

Andros Island, 6

Angkor Wat, 44

Annunciation, 106-108

Anu, 33

Anunnaki, 34

Apocrypha, 34

Apollo 11, 86, 87, 119

Apollo 14, 4

Apollo 17, 5

Apollo 13, 4

Archangels, 106, 108

Area 51, 6

Armstrong, Neil, 5

Asso. for Research & Enlightment, 67

Astronaut Edgar Mitchell, 4

Astronaut Eugene Cernan, 5

Astronaut Gordon Cooper, 5

Astronaut James Lovell, 4

Astronaut John Glenn, 5

Astronaut Neil Armstrong, 5

Astronaut Scott Carpenter, 4

Astronomical Observatory in Bonn, 45

Atahualpa, 40

Atlantean, 26, 66-72

Atlantis (picture), 70

Atlantis, 26, 63-72

Atlas, 63

Aurora, Texas, 3

AUTEC, 6, 7

Avenue of the Dead, 50

Azaz'el, 24

Azazel, 35, 84, 85

Aztecs, 41-53

Babel, 33

Bad-tibira, 35, 84

Baian-Kara-Ula Mountains, 64

Baktun, 92-100

Balducci, Monsignor Corrado, xx, 101

Baptism of Christ, xi, 104, 105, 127

Bassett, Stephen, 5, 6, 117

Bender, Vern, xiii

Bermuda Triangle, 6, 130

Beth-El, 18

Bible, xix-xxii, 10-35, 60, 63, 83-115

Bigfoot sightings (map), 81

Bigfoot, x, 80, 81, 126

Bimini Roads, 71

Black hole, 90, 95

Blind Faith, xix, 111

Blumrich, Josef, 13

Book of Changes, 92

Book of Enoch, xxii, 23, 84, 85, 87, 91, 111, 115

Book of Revelation, 63

Border Cave, South Africa, 34

Bowers, Stephen, 81

Brody, Thomas, 29

Bronze Age, 55, 66

Bruce, James, 23

Brunhes-Matuyama Reversal, 93

Brush Creek Township, Ohio, 81

Buddhism, xx, 69

Butt, Yousaf, 94

Cain, 22

Calendar of Nippur, 32

Canaan, 22

Canon of Scripture, 23

Cape Canaveral, 86

Cardiff in Wales, Great Britain, 2

Carlson, Veda, 71

Carpenter, Scott, 4

Carter, Jimmy, 4

Catholic Church, xx, 11, 78, 101

Cayce, Edgar (picture), 67

Cayce, Edgar, x, 26, 66, 67, 71, 72, 99, 118, 125

Cayuga, 78

Cernan, Eugene, 5

Chabur 13

Chariots of the Gods, xx, 112, 116

Chariots, xxii, 13-16 23, 61, 111, 112, 116,

Charlemagne, 21

Chi Pu Tei, 64

Chichen Itza's Great Ball Court, x, 54-55, 125

Chicxulub Crater, 47

Childress, D.H., 63

Chitty, John, 88, 115

Christianity, iii, xx, xix, 21, 82, 90

Church of Transfiguration, 102

Churchward, James, 69, 70, 126

City of Tenoch, 50, 53

Clement of Alexandria, 23

Clouds, xxii, 13-16, 19, 23, 99, 111

Clovis Culture, 77

Codex Vaticanus, xxi, 51, 115

Collins, Michael, 86

Columbia, 86

Commodianus, 23

Consolmagno, Guy, xx, xxi, 102

Constantine, 21

Cooper, Gordon, 5

Copernicus, Nicolaus, 51

Cortez, Hernan, 40, 50

Coyne, George, 12, 13, 117

Cretno, Michael, 81

Crik, Francis, 109
Crivelli, Carlo, xi, 106, 107, 128
Cro-Magnon man, 38
Cuneiform writing, 31
Cuzco, Peru, ix, 41, 42, 45, 124
Cyrulik, Dave and Kathy, xiii
Cytherean Complex, 29
Daniel, 13, 14, 24, 89, 90, 98, 118
David and Goliath, 77
David, Fred, xvii
David, Joy, Forest, Byron, and Meredith, xiii, xviii
Dead Sea Scrolls, xxi, 115
Death Valley, 77
Delarof, 3
Disciples of Christ, 67
Disclosure Project, 6, 117
Devall, Robert, 27
DNA, 35, 38, 109
Dogon, 64, 65
Draco the Dragon (Satan), 89, 90, 96
Dropa, 64
Dvapara, 63
Eagle, 16, 86, 89
Easter Island, x, 44, 51, 52, 124
Egyptians, xx, 26, 29, 30, 55, 60, 68, 89, 109, 110
Elijah, 13-15, 18, 23, 102-103
Elisha, 13-15, 23
Emim, 77
Emperor Cheng Tang, 64
Emperor Shun, 64
Empire State Building, 28
Enki, 33-34
Enlil, 33

Enmedurannki, 35
Enoch, viii, xx, 22-25, 34, 35, 50, 85, 86, 112, 141
Epic of Gilgamesh, xxi, 34, 115
Eric Von Daniken, xx, 116
Eridu, 31, 35
Eskimos of Greenland, 76
Ethiopian Christian Church, 23
Everhart, George and Shirley, xiii
Everhart, J.F., 81
Evolution, xxi, 38, 84, 109-110
Exodus, ix, 16, 17, 21, 123
Exodus Route (picture), 17
Eyck, Jan van, xi, 107-108, 128
Ezekiel, 13, 14, 18, 20, 35, 92
Ezra, 13-14
Fallen angels, 18, 24, 29, 30, 32, 33, 35, 38, 39, 43, 49, 53, 54, 59, 74, 80, 82-90, 109-110
Feathered Serpent, 48
Fifth Sun, 51, 55
First Crusade, 23
Fitzwilliam Museum, 104, 105, 127
Flood, vii, 21, 36, 58, 73-74, 111, 112, 117
Forbidden Archaeology, 81
Funes, Jose Gabriel, 101
Gabriel, 101, 106, 107
Galactic equator, 56, 95
Gelder, Aert, xi, 104, 105, 127
Geomagnectic reversal, 74
German Astronomical Commission, 45
Ghirlandaio, Domenico, xv
Giant human femur (picture), 79

Giants, vii, xx, xxi, 35, 41-88, 112, 118

Gigantopithecus, 81

Gilgal, 23

Gilgamesh, xxi, 34, 115

Gillette, Randall, xiii

Glenn, John, 5

Global Polarity Timescale (GPTS), 93

God the Father, xxii, 19, 102, 109-111

Gomorroh, 18-19

Government UFO Cover-up, 6-7, 117

Great Ball Court, 54

Great Flood, 36, 73, 117

Great Judgment, 89

Great Pyramid of Cholula, 49

Great Pyramid of Giza Picture, 27

Great Pyramid of Giza, ix, 26, 28, 29, 49, 110

Great Sphinx Picture, 28

Great Sphinx, ix, 28, 89, 123

Greer, Stephen, 6

Groom Lake, Nevada, 6

Habakkuk, 13-14

Hangzhou, China, 1, 104, 117

Hann, Julius, 76, 119-120

Hanselmann, Eric, xiii

HARI gene, 109

Heine, Johan, 34

Hibbon, Frank, 75

Hinduism, xx, 60

Hitler, 61

Hoagland, Richard, 29

Honduras National Museum, 56

Hopi Indians, 56, 92, 111

Hromnik, Cyril, 34

Hubbard, Samuel, 77

Huehuhuetan River, 58, 68

Hyderabad Computer Model, 93

Idrees in Surah Al (The Prophets), 22

Ienaeus, 23

Inca Empire, 40

India, vii, 60-68, 125

India Times, 92

Indus Valley (picture), 62

Indus Valley Civilization, x, 56, 59-65, 125

Isaiah, 13-15, 92

Island of the Moon, 41

Island of the Sun, 41

Isle Royale, 34

Israelites, 17

Izapa, 57

Jacob's Ladder, ix, 19, 20, 123

James, 13, 14, 102

Jebel Musa, 17

Jeremiah, 13, 14, 16

Jericho, 18, 31

Jerusulem, 23, 33

Jesuit, xx, 101-102

Jesus (picture), 113

Jesus, xi, xv, xx, xxii, 13-16, 19-21, 35, 39, 83, 87, 92, 99-106, 110-113, 121, 127, 128

Jewish Encyclopedia, 24

Job, 13-15, 24, 56, 83, 89

Joel, 13-14

John, xx, 13, 14, 16, 83, 102

John the Baptist, 104

Jonah, 13, 14, 111
Jordan River, 104
Joseph, Rhawn, 117
Joshua, 13, 14, 19, 77
Jude, 22, 23, 85
Judgment Day, 85, 89
Justin Martyr, 23
Kalasasaya Pyramid, 44-45
Kennedy, Robert F., 4
Kennett, Douglas, 73
Keweenaw Peninsula, 34
Khabur River, 35
Khafre, 28
Kish, 31, 33
Kiss, Edmund, 44
Knights Templar, 23
Kohlschutter, Arnold, 45
Koosk, Paul, 45
Krishna, 63
Krita, 63
Kueshana, Eklal, 64
Kukulcan, 54
Kurten, Bjorn, 37
Lactantius, 23
Lake Texcoco, 50
Lake Titicaca, x, 40-44, 118, 124
Last Day, vii, xxii, 51, 56, 63, 90-100, 112, 118
Lauzon, Bruce, xiii
Lemuria (picture), 70
Lemuria, x, 64, 69-72, 126
Leo the Lion (Ra), 89
Lhasa Tablets, 69-71
Lion Cavern, South Africa, 34
Lion Coal Mine, 34
Long Count Calendar (picture), 57

Long Count Calendar, x, 55, 57, 72, 125
Loper, David, 93
Lovell, James, 4, 130
Ludendorff, Hans, 45
Luke, 13, 14, 19, 22, 84, 99, 104, 106
Lusar, Rudolf, 61
MacArthur, Douglas, 3
Machu Picchu, Peru, 41, 118, 136
Madonna, 121, 122, ix, xv
Magnetic pole reversal, 76, 93-94
Mahabharata, 61
Mainardi, Sebastiano, xv
Mammoth (picture), 76
Mammoths, x, 75, 76, 126
Marchetti, Victor, 7
Mark, 13-16, 104
Mars, 29, 87, 119, 142
Mary, xv, 16, 106, 107, 121, 127-128
Matlactli Atl, 51
Matthew, 13, 14, 19, 84, 99, 102, 104
Mayan Empire, x, xxi, xxii, 54-58, 71, 89, 92, 99, 100, 118, 125
McKenna, Dennis and Terrence, 92
Meganthropus, 81
Mendelssohn, Kurt, 26
Mesoamerican Long Count Calendar, 55
Mesopotamia, 31
Messiah, 24
Methodius of Philippi, 23
Methuselah, 22
Mexica-Nahuatl, 75

Mexico Map, 49
Milky Way, 90, 95
Minucius Felix, 23
Mitchell, Edgar, 4, 130
Moab, 19
Mohenjo-Daro, 60
Moore Lake, 4
Moses, 13-19, 32, 102, 103
Mount Graham, 102
Mount Tabor (picture), 103
Mount Tabor, 32, 102, 103, 127
Mt. Blanco Fossil Museum, xiii, 77,
    79, 126
Mu, 69-72, 126
Muller, Rolf, 45
Naamah, 84
Nabta, Egypt, 29
Nahul-Ollin, 92
Nahum, 13-14
NASA, 4, 6, 13, 29, 87, 93, 117,
    119
National Gallery, 106
National Gallery of Art, 107
Nazca Drawings, 45-47, 84, 124
Nazca Lines, x, 45-47, 84, 124
Nazi Germany, 61
Neanderthal Picture, 36-37
Neanderthal, ix, 36-38, 80, 123-124
Nefilim, 34
Nehemiah, 13-14
Nephilim, 24, 77,85
New Age Movement, 67
Nippur, 13, 31-35, 84
Noah, 22, 73-74, 82-85
North Pole, x, 74, 96, 98, 118, 127
Not from the Ape, 37

Nu-wah, 74
Oberth, Herman, 3, 4
Ollantaytambu, Peru, 41, 45
Olmec Civilization, x, 48, 49, 53-
    59, 68, 124
Origen, 23
Orion, 27, 29, 65, 89
Orion Project, 6, 117
Osiris, 89
Pacal II, 58-59
Padgett, Jim, xiii
Palenque, 58
Palin, Michael, 41, 118
Papyrus, 31
Patna, 3
Paul, 13-14
Pawnee Indians, 76, 80
Peterson, Joni, xiii
Pegues, Abbe, 77
Pentateuch, 32
Peter, 13, 14, 19, 102, 103
Pharaoh Khafre, 28
Pictographs, 31, 64
Pictun, 92
Pizarro, 40
Plato (picture), 69
Plato, x, 68-72, 125-126
Pleiades, 33, 56, 90
Pole shift or reversal, 74, 76, 93, 96,
    99, 100, 118
Pope John Paul II, 13
Popol Vuh, xxi, 56-59, 68, 91, 116
Posnansky, Arthur, 44-45
Precession of the Equinoxes, 96
Precession, 96, 99, 118
President Jimmy Carter, 4

Public Acclimation Program, 101
Pulkovo Observatory, 96
Puma Punku, Peru, 43-45, 72
Purple Mountain Astronomical
    Observatory, 1
Qasr at-Yahud, 105
Pyramid of the Moon, 50
Pyramid of the Sun, 50
Pyramids on Venus, 29
Quetzalcoatl, 48-54
Quran, 13, 22, 108, 116
Rama Empire, 64
Ramirez, Ed, xiii
Red Sea, 21, 111
Reich, David, 38
Reiche, Maria, 45, 124
Rephaim, 77
Resurrection, 21, 111-112
Revelation (Book of), 63, 88, 89
Roman Catholic Church, xx, 11
Roman Empire, 21, 23
Roswell, New Mexico, 3, 4
Ruta, 64
Sacsahuaman, Peru, 41, 45
Sagittarius A, 95
Sahara, 29
Sala d'Ercole Museum, xv
Samaranga Sutradhara, 62
Samiaza, 84
Samuel, 13, 14, 77
Samyaza, 85-86
Sanderson, Ivan, 63
Sanskrit, 60, 62
Santa Claus, 4, 90
Sasquatch, x, 80, 81, 126

Satan, xx-xxii, 18, 21-24, 33-35, 53-
    59, 83-93, 110-111
Saxons, 21
Schulten, Maria, 41
Sea of Tranquility, 86
Second Coming, 13
Second Pyramid at Giza, 28
Seven Sisters, 33, 56
Sheffield, England, 9
Shems, 33
Sigiburg, 21
Sirius B, 27, 29, 64, 65
Sirius A, 27, 29, 64, 65, 90
Skull comparison (picture), 37
Sky thrones, 13
Sleeping Prophet, 26, 66
Smock, Bob and Joan, xiii
Soddy, Frederick, 61
Sodom, 18-19
Solar flare (picture), 94
Solar flares, x, 93, 94, 100, 126
Solar storm, 93-94
Soloman's Temple, 23
Solomon, 13, 14, 123
Son of man, 83, 87
Son of Man, xxi, 14, 15, 99, 102
Sons of God, vii, xx, 24, 38, 77, 82-
    89, 112, 116, 141
South Africa, 34, 35, 84
Spitsberger, 98
Squier, Ephraim George, 42
St. Christopher, 78
Stone Age, 55, 84
Stonehenge, x, 51-52, 56, 124
Straits of Gibraltar, 68
Sumatra, Indonesia, 47, 72

Sumeria map, 32
Sumerian civilization, 33, 74
Sunspots, 93-94
Supreme Council of Antiquities, 29
Surah Maryam (Mary), 22
Svalbard Global Seed Vault, 97-98, 127
Tatian, 23
Taurus, 33
Taylor, Joe, xiii, 79, 126
Tell Brak, 35
Temple of Inscriptions, 58
Tenochtitlan, 50, 53
Teotihuacan, 50, 53
Tertullian, 23
The Atlantis Encyclopedia, 66, 116
The Broken Bible, 88, 115
The Great Migration, 71
Thomas Bannan Astrophysics Facility, 12
Thompson, Richard, 81
Tiahuanacu, Peru, 41-45, 84
Tigris and Euphrates rivers, 31, 74
Toba volcanic eruption, 47, 72
Toltecs, 49
Tongue of the Ocean, 6
TOTO, 6
Tower of Babel, iii, 33
Transfiguration, 102-103, 112, 127
Treta, 63
Trinity, xxi, 102, 109
Troana Codex, 71
True People, 54
Tsum Um Nui, 64
Tunguska , Siberia, 95

Twelve, 29, 35, 41, 46, 60, 71, 75, 86, 108, 109
Tyre, a Phoenician city, 20, 31
Uffizi Gallery, 104
UFO picture, 2, 9, 105, 106
UFO-Atlantis Connection, 65-72
UFO-Aztec Connection, vii, 48-53
UFO-*Bible* Connection, vii, 10-21
UFO-Christianity Connection, vii, xvii, xix, xxi, xxii, 21, 25, 29, 53, 59, 65, 72, 76, 100-113
UFO-Egypt Connection, vii, 26-30
UFO-Enoch Connection, vii, 22-25
UFO-Flood Connection, vii, 73-76
UFO-Giant Connection, vii, 77-82
UFO-Inca Connection, vii, 40-47
UFO-India Connection, vii, 60-65
UFO-Last Day Connection, vii, 91-100
UFO-Maya Connection, vii, 53-59
UFO-Sons of God Connection, vii, 83-87
UFO-Sumerian Connection, vii, 31-39
UFO-Underworld Connection, vii, 88-90
UFOs, 1, 2, 9, 105, 106
Underworld, vii, xx-xxii, 22, 24, 29, 30, 39, 42, 56, 59, 80-93, 110, 111
Unidentified Flying Objects, 1-10, 105-106
Uriel, 22, 24, 85-86
U.S.S. *Vulture,* 3
Vailixi, 64

Vatican Advanced Technology Telescope (VATT), 12
Vatican Observatory (picture and) Research Group, 12
Vatican Observatory, xx, 11, 12, 102, 117, 123
Vatican, ii, xx, xxi, 12, 21, 45, 101, 102, 110, 111, 115
Vedas, xxi, 60-68, 72, 116
Venus Complex, 29
Venus, 29
Veracruz, 48, 57
Verrochio, Andrea del, 104
Viking photographs of Mars, 29
Vimana Aircraft of Ancient India and Atlantis, 60-64
Vimanas, 60-64
Vinci, Leonardo da, 104
Viracocha, 40-46
Vrishnis, 61
Wade, Richard, 34
Watchers, 110-111
Wheels, 3, 13, 57
Whirlwinds, 13-18, 23
Williams, Bruce and Kathy, xiii
Winter solstice of 2012, 56, 59, 98
Wise Men, 19, 21, 111
Wobble, 51, 56, 59, 95
Wonder Weapons, 61
Wright, Orville and Wilbur, 47
Xelhua, 49
Xiaoshan Airport UFO sighting, 1, 104, 117
Yahew, 34
Yamantau Mountain Complex, x, 96, 97, 126

Yellowstone National Park, 47
Yephaniah, 13, 14
Yeti, 80
Yolke, Bolton, 56
Younger Dryas, 73
Yucutan Peninsula, 47
Zechariah, 13-15, 116
Zeus, 33, 74
Zimmerman, Michael, 35, 118
Zulu, 35, 84